THE
WHISKY
WORLD TOUR

A curated guide to
unforgettable distilleries
and their whiskies

JOEL HARRISON

Foreword by Charles MacLean

MITCHELL BEAZLEY

Contents

The Tour

Foreword

by Charles MacLean, M.B.E., Master of the Quaich

The task Joel Harrison has set himself in this book is formidable – no less than a worldwide whisky tour of the very best distilleries to visit around the globe.

It is impossible for such a book to be comprehensive – whisky is produced in 87 countries; new distilleries are licensed every week and all the 'traditional' producing countries (Scotland, Ireland, the USA, Canada and Japan) have expanded capacity significantly. So Joel's pick of distilleries is necessarily selective. He has chosen wisely, not only including distilleries from the five leading whisky countries but also newcomers from Scandinavia to South Africa, China to New Zealand and India. Household names have been included, but also the lesser-known, more recently established sites. The only constraint Joel acknowledges is that each listing should welcome visitors.

Until the late 1960s, whisky making was shrouded in secrecy. Distilleries were industrial sites and the thought of allowing members of the public through the gates was anathema. Within the mighty Distillers Company Limited (DCL) – which in 1980 owned 43 malt whisky distilleries – workers at any one site were forbidden from discussing their operation with those at any other site within the group.

It was the growing interest in malt whisky that encouraged owners to open their distilleries to the public. The independently run William Grant & Sons was the pioneer: in July 1969 it converted an old malt barn into a reception area at the Glenfiddich distillery, installed a shop and began to conduct guided tours. Charles Gordon, the company's chairman, remarked: 'Glenfiddich was becoming much more popular, so it was a natural thing to do. Also we were aware that DCL and Seagram didn't allow people into their distilleries and wouldn't allow photographs to be taken in case the Japanese copied what they were doing.'

Not far behind was James Fairlie, who bought the small and picturesque Glenturret distillery, Crieff, in 1957 with the revolutionary idea of displaying the craft of whisky-making to interested parties. As early as 1964, Fairlie had shown Sir Alec Douglas-Home, the then Prime Minister of the UK, around 'the works'. Soon after, the distillery began to welcome coach loads of people on tours of 'Rob Roy Country'.

Visiting Distilleries, published in 2001, was the first guide of its kind; it listed 41 sites that welcomed visitors at the time. Today, there are more than 70 open to the public, and a further 10 by appointment. 'Whisky tourism' is now Scotland's leading visitor attraction, with more than two million visits recorded annually.

Across the Irish Sea, meanwhile, Irish distillers have long operated 'whiskey tourism' venues at opposite ends of the Irish Republic. Dublin is home to the original Jameson distillery, while in County Cork, the 'old' Midleton distillery provides a glimpse into Irish distilling in days gone by. George Roe's distillery in Dublin closed in 1926 but an impressive visitor's centre opened on the site in 2022. In Northern Ireland, Bushmills distillery on the Antrim Coast has welcomed the public for many years.

These attractions have now been joined by a 'new wave' of distilleries offering visitor facilities. Most of them are featured on the Irish Whiskey Trail, which also highlights some of the country's best bars. The Irish Whiskey Tourism Strategy, a campaign published in 2016, set an ambitious target of attracting 1.7 million visitors to Irish distilleries within a decade.

In the USA, there is the designated Kentucky Bourbon Trail which embraces 18 distilleries. In the state capital of Louisville, which has seen a revitalization of distilling operations and associated visitor attractions in recent years, there is the Urban Bourbon Trail. It highlights no fewer than 46 bars and restaurants that place bourbon centre stage. Tennessee, Kentucky's great 'whiskey state' rival, will not be outdone: it promotes distilling activities across 26 venues via The Tennessee Whiskey Trail.

'Whisky tourism' is certainly not confined to the traditional distilling nations, with many sites around the world welcoming visitors. In Taiwan, Kavalan, which was established in 2005, regularly plays host to more than one million people each year.

In *The Whisky World Tour*, Joel makes for a cheerful and knowledgeable travelling companion. His accounts of each distillery are personal and full of entertaining stories – and there is no spirit on earth more 'storied' than whisky – as well as being informative, inspirational and even lyrical at times. This book is an essential addition to any whisky library.

Introduction

The world of whisky is steeped in rich histories, distinct geographies, and the subtle art of distillation and maturation. When you pull the stopper out of a bottle of whisky, you are uncorking history, pouring the past and sipping on stories.

A glass of whisky is a ritual, an experience. The 'who, where and why' of whisky is what makes this spirit so special and allows it to stand out from other drinks. Every whisky distillery, whether founded when records were handwritten or with a flurry of social media posts, is steeped in a blend of narratives – and visiting these hallowed sites is a real pilgrimage.

My own pilgrimage started 20 years ago, at the tail end of winter, when I found myself on the remote, windswept Scottish island of Islay. I was drawn there by the distinctly smoky single malt the isle is famed for. In the rugged landscape, where the air is thick with the scent of peat smoke and the Atlantic's waves crash against rocky shores, I experienced a genuine sense of place that perfectly framed the isle's famous malts.

Such is the visceral, elemental nature of Islay whisky, it was as if I'd been there

before. Visiting for the first time added an extra layer of depth to my whisky-drinking experience. Even now, just a waft of the earthy aroma from an Islay whisky has the power to transport me back to the pier at Port Ellen, the harbour at Bowmore or the beguiling view of neighbouring Jura from the banks of the Caol Ila distillery.

Since then, in my capacity as a whisky writer, I have been privileged to travel across the world and visit distilleries that have chosen not to make their spirit in the shadows, but to throw their doors open and embrace you, me and anyone else who wants to look behind the curtain and see the magic of the spirit in motion. This book is a guide to the very best whisky experiences around the world.

The journey laid out in the following pages starts in North America, taking in Canadian and American frontier distillers in states such as Colorado and Texas, before hitting famous names in Kentucky and Tennessee – the distilleries which stand as monuments to American innovation and resilience. In the heart of bourbon country, vast tracts of rolling land are occupied by the likes of Maker's Mark and Buffalo Trace. Each distiller in these bluegrass fields is a chapter in the grand story of American whiskey, and America itself, their doors open for you to explore.

We then hop over to Ireland where places such as Bushmills in the north and the Old Jameson distillery in Dublin are flag-bearers for Irish whiskey. Wherever you find yourself on the Emerald Isle, you will be welcomed into the fold in a land famed for its warmth and hospitality, a fact showcased in each of the Irish distilleries featured in this book.

A detailed look at Scotland is required, too. Not just of key producers on Islay but of distilleries in other islands. In regions such as Speyside and the Highlands, the story of whisky is the richest and brightest thread in the country's tartan-like, colourful history.

I make no apologies for Scotch distilleries having the largest percentage of this book. It is Scottish distilleries that pioneered the visitor experience and continue to invest heavily in the truism that Scotch is much more than a malt spirit matured in cask; it is

time itself, the history, people and place that makes their drink so special.

Continuing around the world, we look at the best whisky producers internationally who are willing to welcome you into their homes. From England to Australia, with a layover in China, whisky distilleries have opened their gates, warehouses, casks and bottles for you to visit, taste, try and enjoy. Why have they done this? Because whisky is more than a drink. It is a convivial conversation, an experience distilled.

Finally, on the other side of the world from where we began, Japan offers a fascinating contrast. Here, meticulous attention to detail and reverence for tradition are taken to an almost spiritual level. The distilleries of The Yamazaki and Hakushu are temples of precision, where whisky is an art and a craft that's treated with the same dedication that goes into a fine tea ceremony. The Japanese approach is both disciplined and innovative, blending the best of Eastern and Western techniques to create something truly extraordinary.

So, pour yourself a glass, sit back and let's embark on this worldwide whisky tour of the very best distilleries to visit around the globe. May your travels be spirited and your glasses ever full.

Cheers!

@joeldram

How this book works

The Whisky World Tour is not designed to be an exhaustive list of whisky distilleries around the globe, nor is this a fully detailed guide to distilling. Should you be after a wonderfully researched and exhaustive guide to the world's whisky distilleries, I will point you in the direction of Dave Broom's *World Atlas of Whisky*. Now in its third edition, it does what no other publication has done, which is to compile as complete a guide to the growing global whisky scene as is possible.

If you are in the market for a guide to whisky distilling, you can flip forward a couple of pages where I'll guide you through the basics of making different styles of whisky. A manual to distilling, however, this is not.

This book is your ticket to 52 of the best whisky distilleries to visit across the globe, but let's be clear: this isn't about hitting up some postcard-perfect tourist traps. This is about getting under the skin of each distillery, understanding what makes them tick and, most importantly, figuring out why you should care.

This romp around the world of whisky is broken down into sections of North America, Ireland, Scotland, Rest of the

World and Japan. Each starts with a dispatch from the place; a short overview that details what makes the whisky from these areas unique, a history of whisky-making in these places and a look at the best times to visit.

Then the journey starts: 52 focus distilleries, each brought to life through their history, craftsmanship and, of course, their whisky. You'll discover what makes each distillery unique, from its location and heritage to the specific techniques that influence its distinctive flavours. The history will provide insight into the origins of each distillery, the people behind it and how they've maintained traditions or innovated in modern times.

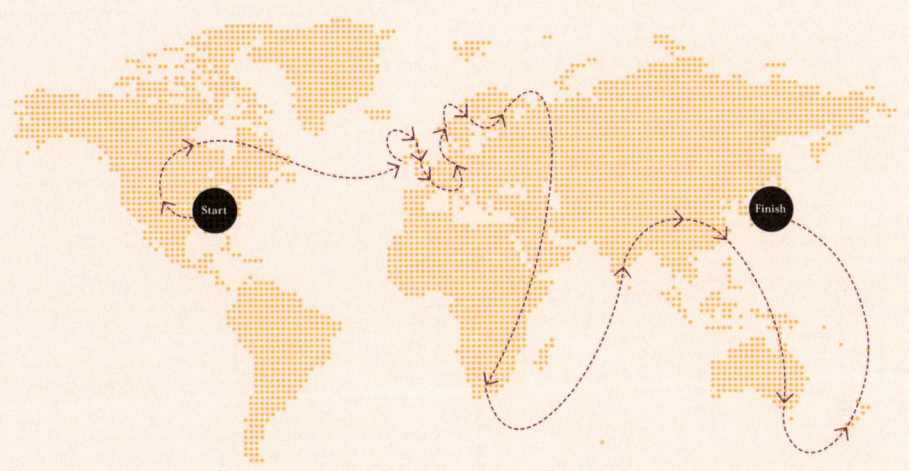

These distilleries aren't just places where whisky is made; they're cultural landmarks, places where generations of craft and tradition collide with new ideas and experimentation. While a physical visit to these locations might be a dream for many, this book allows you to immerse yourself in the essence of these distilleries.

But you don't have to board a plane or stamp your passport to follow along. With 52 profiles (one a week for a year), this book is designed to let you experience these distilleries from the comfort of your couch or, better yet, your favourite barstool. For those looking to visit these distilleries virtually, tasting notes are included for some of the core range whiskies.

You'll be able to taste as you read, by picking up a bottle at your local shop or seeking out samples. By the end of the year, you'll have travelled the world of whisky, gaining new knowledge, experiences and perhaps even a few new favourites along the way.

Ultimately, *The Whisky World Tour* isn't just a guidebook, it's an invitation to expand your palate and your horizons. When you're done, you'll know your whisky a little better, you'll know the people behind it a little better and maybe, just maybe, you'll know yourself a little better, too.

What makes a good whisky distillery trip?

Let us consider the experience of visiting a distillery – as this is what the book is all about. The first question to start with is 'why'. Why visit a distillery at all when it brings the ultimate experience – its whisky – to us?

Well, visiting a whisky distillery, approached in the proper spirit, is one of the more edifying pursuits one can undertake. There is, of course, the promise of a dram or two at the end, which is always a powerful incentive. It also offers the chance to see where, why and by whom these whiskies are made. That is the real attraction.

In the pursuit of whisky education, you will read – and be told many times over (including later in this very book) – that whisky is made from water, grains/cereals, a little bit of yeast, and time maturing in wood. All this is true in the most basic of senses, in the same way that a human is made of carbon, or that we share 80 per cent of our DNA with bananas, or mice, or some such. This is of course utterly correct, but at the same time complete nonsense. As humans we are made up of so much more, and it is the 'more' – our spirit, soul and personality – that makes us who we are.

This is also true for whisky. It is not just a process and product, a brand and 'brand home' (as you will hear distillery visitor's centres referred to). Each whisky, be it a single malt Scotch, an American bourbon, an Irish pot still whiskey or any others from around the globe, is rooted in the people who make it, and the place it is made. It is nature and nurture as one.

This is the first tip for visiting any distillery: look beyond the liquid and gaze through the glass to what is really important – the sense of place and the importance of people. This is the single best reason to visit any distillery, anywhere in the world.

The second is to learn. Each distillery will have its own process and product, often born from centuries of trial and error. There is not one distillery I have been to where I've not come away having learned something new, or refined my knowledge further still. The old adage that, 'every day is a school day' rings true. And when you are at a distillery, ask questions. 'Why do you ferment for longer than others? Why did the distillery close for 25 years? Do you worry about earthquakes?' These sorts of things.

At the very best visitor's centres, these questions are often answered before the tour even starts, by wonderful, exotic and sometimes high-tech presentations, videos or projections, plotting the brand's history and narrative. At others, there is a simpler, people-powered approach with a tour guide as your point of contact, ready and willing to answer your probing questions.

One thing to remember is that whisky is historically an agricultural pursuit. It was born in the glens of Scotland, or the valleys of Ireland and on the farms of Kentucky and Tennessee. What this means for today's visitors is that often these now famed sites are not in the centre of cities, or even in well-connected towns, but hidden away in remote areas.

Therefore, some planning is key. Take the wonderful island of Islay, for example. The Inner Hebridean island is home to a whopping 11 distilleries, with more to open. But there are only a few flights a day from Glasgow, and with limited capacity. The regular-ish ferry, which takes nearly three hours, is another three hours' drive from Glasgow (if the roads are open). Once on the island, bus routes are scarce and accommodation is often fully booked. But don't let this put you off. With some forethought, flights are easily booked, or car hire and ferry tickets secured. Accommodation is bookable in advance and you'll find an island welcoming to all who want to visit, with locals often stopping to pick up rain-drenched hikers walking from distillery to distillery.

If you are driving (I challenge you to find another way to get to, say, Jack Daniel's or Nearest Green in Tennessee), note that often 'drivers' drams', the samples at tastings filled into small bottles to take-away, are offered.

Finally, let's talk about the whisky itself, as this is the real reason anyone wants to visit their favourite distillery. Each visit should enhance the connection between drinker and dram. The location should become manifest when sipping next to the still from which the spirit has been made. This, if I'm honest, is the single biggest draw for me. It is like seeing a band play in their home city; there is something extra special about it. Many whisky distilleries will also offer unique bottlings to those willing to make the trip, and these souvenirs are designed to reward, surprise and delight. So if you get the chance to pick one up, do.

In the end, a great distillery visit will leave you with more than just a warm whisky buzz. You'll walk away with a connection to the land, the people and the tradition behind the bottle you take home. And when you pour yourself a glass weeks, months, or even years later, you'll remember that day; the smell of the maturing barrels, the stories shared and the taste of something made with patience and passion.

What is whisky?

Put in the most basic of terms, whisky is a spirit that is distilled from fermented grains or cereals, and matured in wood. Of course, this is a wide description. When thinking about whisky, we are most commonly looking at Irish pot still, Scottish single malt or American bourbon. All of these have their own strict definitions, history, process and sense of place.

Yet, despite all these differences, whisky is a family with a distinct DNA of flavour. If you like single malt Scotch, you'll probably like bourbon, and you'll certainly like Japanese malt whisky.

Of course, some whisky is famed for its age: Scotch, most notably, matures well into old age – it is not uncommon for distilleries to have expressions up to and beyond 30 years of age – while others, such as bourbon, are often bottled before they have reached double figures.

Grains

The base grain from which whisky is produced differs and is mostly rooted in the locality of the distillery. Single malts, wherever they are distilled, will be made solely from malted barley, which is relatively easy to ferment. Malted barley is often used in small amounts to aid the fermentation of other grains such as wheat, corn, rye and – in Ireland – unmalted barley.

Corn (or maize) is the second major cereal used in whisky production. It is predominantly seen in American bourbon and Canadian whiskies. By law in America, bourbon whiskey must be made with at least 51 per cent corn. It is also used for 'grain whisky', made for blending at more industrial sites across countries such as Scotland and Japan. The Chita distillery, which produces the grain whisky element for the Japanese Hibiki blend, uses corn, for example. Corn needs to be treated differently to malted barley and is often pressure-cooked to help release the starches that turn into sugar and finally alcohol in the fermentation process.

Another important grain in whisky production is rye. This small but powerful grain gives a spicy, almost earthy note (think rye bread), either as the predominant cereal or as part of a 'mash bill', the recipe used by bourbon distillers. When used in bourbon production, it adds a kick of intense flavour.

One less commonly used headline cereal, but one that delivers a highly prized smoothness, is wheat. Seen mostly in American whiskey production, it gives a rich, creamy and slightly nutty note.

Other cereals can be used, including oats (see Midleton distillery, page 82), buckwheat, millet and spelt but these are rare. All this highlights one key question that you should always ask when visiting any distillery: 'What is your base grain, or mash bill?'

Smoke

One of the common misconceptions of Scotch is that it is always smoky. In fact, the majority of whisky made in Scotland is unpeated or unsmoked. The small amount of single malts that are, however, have an incredibly loyal following.

The smoky notes in any whisky are made by the burning of peat (earth that has formed under pressure over thousands of years) under malted barley, with the smoke leaving an indelible mark on the grain.

Peat bogs are found across Scotland and, usually, local peat is used. This gives subtle differences in the flavour imparted. For example, Highland Park (see page 176) has a lighter, heathery style than Islay's Port Ellen (see page 116). Even smoky malts from Japan

and India will often use imported smoked malt from Scotland for the quality and flavour profile.

Occasionally, you will find whisky smoked in other ways, but these are very rare indeed. When visiting a whisky distillery, you should be able to smell the peat smoke in the air, if its whisky is made in this manner. You won't find this style in Kentucky or Tennessee, but it is always worth asking at a single malt distillery, anywhere in the world, if it uses peated malt or not. You'll find most, even those with an entirely unpeated core range, will produce a small run of smoky whisky once a year.

Fermentation and distillation

We have our grain/cereal, from which each distillery will produce a 'beer', or 'wash'. This mixture, at about 7 to 8 per cent ABV, is the result of the grains soaking in hot water that is either filtered (in the case of single malt) or not (in the case of bourbon). Yeast is then added to turn the sugars washed out from the grains into alcohol. This process is key and the length of time that any distillery ferments for will have a massive effect on the final flavour of its spirit.

The longer the fermentation, the fruiter the spirit style will be. It is always a good question to ask about the distillery's wash style and fermentation times. Some distilleries can ferment for well over three days, and many smaller producers will leave their wash to develop further over weekends and holidays.

After alcohol and flavour has been developed with fermentation, it is time to distil. This is a simple process whereby the water and alcohol are separated by boiling the 'beer' or 'wash', as alcohol evaporates at a lower temperature than water.

Most single malt distilleries use traditional copper pot stills for this task; here, size matters. Bigger, taller stills will often create a lighter, more floral spirit, such as the ones at Glenmorangie (see page 172). Smaller stills, for which The Macallan is famed (see page 156), give a more robust style of malt spirit.

Nearly all single malt whisky distilleries will be consistent in their still sizes and shapes, as they want to focus on making their own individual style of spirit. However, if you visit the still room at The Yamazaki in Japan (see page 232), you'll find a variety of different shapes and sizes, allowing the distillery to produce a spectrum of styles of spirit.

The other style of still, which is more often found in bourbon production, is the column still. These are tall stills made of copper or stainless steel plates. As the spirit vapours pass up through the column, the plates condense the vapours back into liquid. These plates are, in effect, a series of mini-distillations. The taller the still – and the more plates – the 'purer' the spirit produced. In bourbon, you might hear about a 'thumper' or a 'doubler', which is an extra chamber (like a small pot still) attached to the final column. This too will have an impact on the spirit style from each distillery.

As well as their stills, always ask a distillery about their condensers, the element that brings the spirit vapours back to a liquid. Particularly in single malt, the condenser will have another effect on the final flavour of the distillery's spirit. 'Worm tubs' and 'shell and tube' (see page 17) are the most common condensers, both giving different results.

Maturation

Whisky is predominantly matured in wooden casks. In Europe and the UK, it is a legal requirement that any bottle that carries the term 'whisky' (with or without the 'e') must be matured in wood for a minimum of three years and one day. This is not the case in other parts of the world. Bourbon, for example, has no minimum age in cask. Therefore, it cannot be sold in Europe as 'whiskey' if it is under three years old.

The goal of maturation is to bring colour and flavour to the whisky. Oak, the favoured style for casks, is a porous material that lends itself to ideal maturation. In America, bourbon must be matured in brand new oak casks, which gives an intense oak spice and full flavour to this style of whiskey.

For longer maturation in other parts of the world, it is advantageous to employ casks that have already been used for American bourbon or for fortified wines. A pre-used cask will impart less oak notes, so can be used for longer without the tannins from the oak or wood type overpowering the subtle notes of the spirit inside.

The atmosphere in which whisky matures is as close as we get to any sort of terroir in whisky. If the atmosphere is warm and dry, this will have a different effect on the maturation over a climate that is cool and damp. Even within countries, this can differ. At The Macallan, in the Scottish Highlands, thin-walled warehouses encourage the weather in. At Highland Park in the northern Orkney Islands, the distillery's thick stone warehouse walls are designed to keep the wild weather out and maintain a constant temperature inside. In Kentucky, despite the warm summer weather, some distilleries will artificially heat their rack houses to encourage faster, more active maturation.

As casks mature, they will (on the whole) lose a small amount of liquid each year to evaporation. At the Midleton distillery in County Cork, Ireland, the equivalent of around 60,000 bottles of whiskey is lost to evaporation each day. This is known as the 'angels' share'. In Scotland, the average is around 2 per cent a year but in some hot countries, this can be as much as 10 per cent annually. So you can see why this is such a hot topic, if you will...

The world of casks is yet another area where distillers can play tunes with flavour. The difference between single malt Scotch matured in a first fill (which means the first time the Scotch distiller has used it) former Oloroso sherry barrel with a third fill former bourbon barrel will be immense.

The former will give lots of rich nutty notes and a deep red hue to the whisky, and probably only needs a decade or so to reach full maturity. The latter will give little flavour to the whisky and when it does they will be light honey notes, vanilla and green apple. These casks are ideal for extra-long ageing. Some distilleries will move liquid between casks, 'finishing' their whisky in more active, less used and highly flavoursome casks for an extra taste boost.

It is key to ask distilleries about their warehousing and cask programme, as well as their 'angels' share' as it will have a huge impact on their style. You may even be invited in to see, smell or taste the whisky directly from a maturing cask. What a treat!

Essential terms for visiting a whisky distillery

Walking through a distillery tour, these are the terms, equipment and processes that you will typically encounter.

During the Tour: Arrival and History

Distillery Name: Not always the same as on the whisky bottles. Often named after the place (Port Ellen), a person (James Sedgwick), or a brand (Wild Turkey).

Founded: Date of foundation. In many Scottish distilleries, if the date is around 1824 then this is when the distiller was 'caught in the act' by the Crown and forced into purchasing a licence to distil.

Mothballed/Ghosted: When a distillery has been closed for a period.

Pagoda: The 'fluted' roof of a distillery. Formerly the chimney for the floor malting, they are now mostly a design feature.

Silent Season: The period when a distillery is closed for cleaning and essential maintenance. Often just once a year.

During the Tour: Production

New Make/White Dog (US): Whisky spirit before maturation.

Wash: Fermented grains, like beer, pre-distillation.

Mashbill: Recipe of grains/cereals used.

Sourmash/Backset: Resided from the first distillation, added back into the mash. All bourbon and Tennessee whiskey uses this method.

Reflux: Spirit being forced back down a still, to work harder to become vapour, before it is condensed back into liquid. This usually creates a lighter style of spirit.

Draff: Leftover grains after mashing. Often sold as cattle feed.

Yeast: Living microorganisms, used to convert (ferment) sugar into alcohol. By-products are carbon dioxide and heat, both of which are useful commodities to the distiller. The style of yeast used and the length of fermentation will play a significant role in the style of whisky produced.

Oregon Pine: The wood often used for washbacks. They can hide bacteria which are useful in the fermentation of some whiskies.

Cut Point: The strength at which a distillery will 'save' its spirit run-off, discarding the heads and tails. This becomes the style for which a single malt distillery is known.

Spirit Safe: Often made of copper, where the spirit runs through and 'cuts' are made.

In Scotland and Ireland these were often kept locked with only a Government appointed excise officer holding the key.

Condenser: The item that turns the vapours in distillation back into a liquid. The style is very important (see: worm tubs, shell and tube).

Direct-Fired: When stills are heated by flames. This can produce 'hot spots' and caramelization in the stills, adding to flavour complexity.

Steam Jacket: A way of heating stills through steam.

Feints/Tails/Aftershots: The unusable last portion of liquid collected at the end of the last distillation run in a pot still. These can be re-distilled or discarded.

Floor Malting: Traditionally where a distillery would have malted its own barley. Rarely used today.

Peat/Peated: Peat is compressed and semi-carbonized vegetation. When burnt to dry barley in the malt process, the smoke emitted sticks to and flavours the grain. Different peat sources will leave different styles of smoke flavouring. Peated whiskies carry a peat smoke flavour. Smoke is measured in Parts Per Million, or PPM. The higher the PPM, the smokier the whisky.

Kiln: The oven in which peat, or other substances, are burned to create the heat which dries out barley after the process of malting (pictured on page 13).

Lyne Arm: Connects the still to the condenser. The length and angle of the lyne arm will play an impact on spirit style and flavour.

Maltings: Industrial version of floor maltings.

Pot Still: Large, often kettle- or onion-shaped stills (pictured left).

Column Still: Tall stills made up of many plates and often used in bourbon or grain distilling.

Saladin Box: A style of malting, performed in a large box and turned mechanically.

Washbacks: The vessels where the wash or beer is fermented. Made from stainless steel or Oregon pine; the latter hiding bacteria which can be useful in the fermentation process.

Wort: Sweet liquid, which comes from the mash tun, post-filtration. Goes on to have yeast added for fermentation.

Worm Tubs: Traditional method to condense vapour during distillation back to liquid. Coiled spiral tubes which are immersed in cold water. Less copper contact than shell and tube gives a weightier, heavier spirit.

Shell and Tube: An enclosed vessel containing many small copper pipes, filled with cold water. As the vapour from distillation passes through, it condenses onto the copper pipes and forms as a liquid. Develops a lighter spirit than worm tubs.

Capacity: The amount of whisky spirit a distillery can make in a year. Distilleries rarely produce their maximum capacity.

During the Tour: In the Warehouse

Oak/European Oak/American Oak: The main wood type used for maturation.

Barrel/Butt/Cask/Hogshead/Port Pipe/Wine Barrique/Quarter Cask: Size and styles of casks. In bourbon production, brand new barrels (ASB = American Standard Barrels) are exclusively used.

Heads/Foreshots: The ends of a cask. Up to 40 per cent of the surface area of a cask is the 'heads' on either end.

Mizunara: Japanese oak. Highly sought after.

Charring/Char Level/Toasting: Casks are burnt on the inside to release the tannins and lignin, and other flavour components hidden in the wood (pictured below). The higher the level of charr, the greater the impact of flavour on the whisky. Toasted casks are lightly burned.

First Fill/Second Fill/Refill/Finishing: The number of times a cask is used. When

maturing bourbon, a new cask may only be used once. In single malt producing regions, a 'first-fill cask' relates to the first time the distiller has used it, despite the cask having previously held sherry, bourbon or another beverage.

Angels' Share: The loss from casks during maturation. In Scotland, this averages at a compound of 2 per cent per year. In places such as India, it can be up to 10 per cent per annum.

Dunnage Warehouse: Traditional stone walled warehouses where casks are only stacked two or three high and sit on their sides.

Palletized warehouse: Huge warehouses with casks stacked on pallets sitting on their ends.

Rick House: Large warehouses, often in American whiskey production, where casks are stored on their sides.

Cooperage: The part of a distillery where casks are either made from scratch or repaired. Run by coopers.

Filling Strength: The proof or ABV at which distilleries fill their casks. In Scotland, this is traditionally 63.5 per cent. This is an historic strength that makes taxation clearer when trading casks for blends.

Still House: The area of the distillery where the stills are.

Valinch/Copper Dog: Both traditional devices for withdrawing spirit from a cask.

During the Tour: At the Tasting

ABV/Proof: The amount of alcohol in whisky. Expressed as a percentage via ABV (alcohol by volume), or as 'proof' in the US, a traditional system of measuring alcohol

where proof is twice the ABV (aka 50 per cent ABV = 100 proof).

Age Statement/No Age Statement (NAS): The age stated, or not, of a whisky.

Straight Whiskey: American bourbon aged for two years or more.

Bottled In Bond: American bourbon aged for four years or more, and the product of a single season (January to June, or July to December), bottled at 100 proof (50 per cent ABV) and from a single distiller at a single distillery.

Dram: An unspecified measure of whisky.

Driver's Dram: Takeaway samples for drivers.

Cask Strength: The undiluted strength of a whisky when taken directly from a cask.

Chill Filtration: A process where whisky is filtered to remove fatty acids, which can cause a cloudy effect when water is added.

Single Cask: Whisky drawn from one single cask.

Distillery Character: The presence of the house character of the distillery in a whisky. This can be lost with over-ageing or over-active casks, but can be too present in under-matured whisky.

Nosing Glass: A whisky tasting glass designed for the assessment of spirit, often featuring a fluted top.

In the Visitor's Centre Shop

Barrel Pick: In bourbon, a bottle chosen by a bar, store or other organization that's bottled as a single cask.

Distillery Exclusive: A bottling only available at a distillery.

Bottle Your Own/Fill Your Own: A bottle which you can hand-fill at the distillery direct from a cask.

13
...to
Ireland
3–10
1
11–12
Start
2

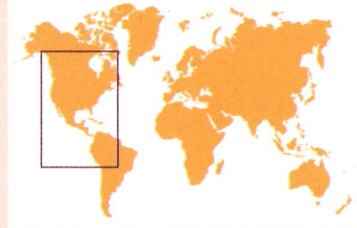

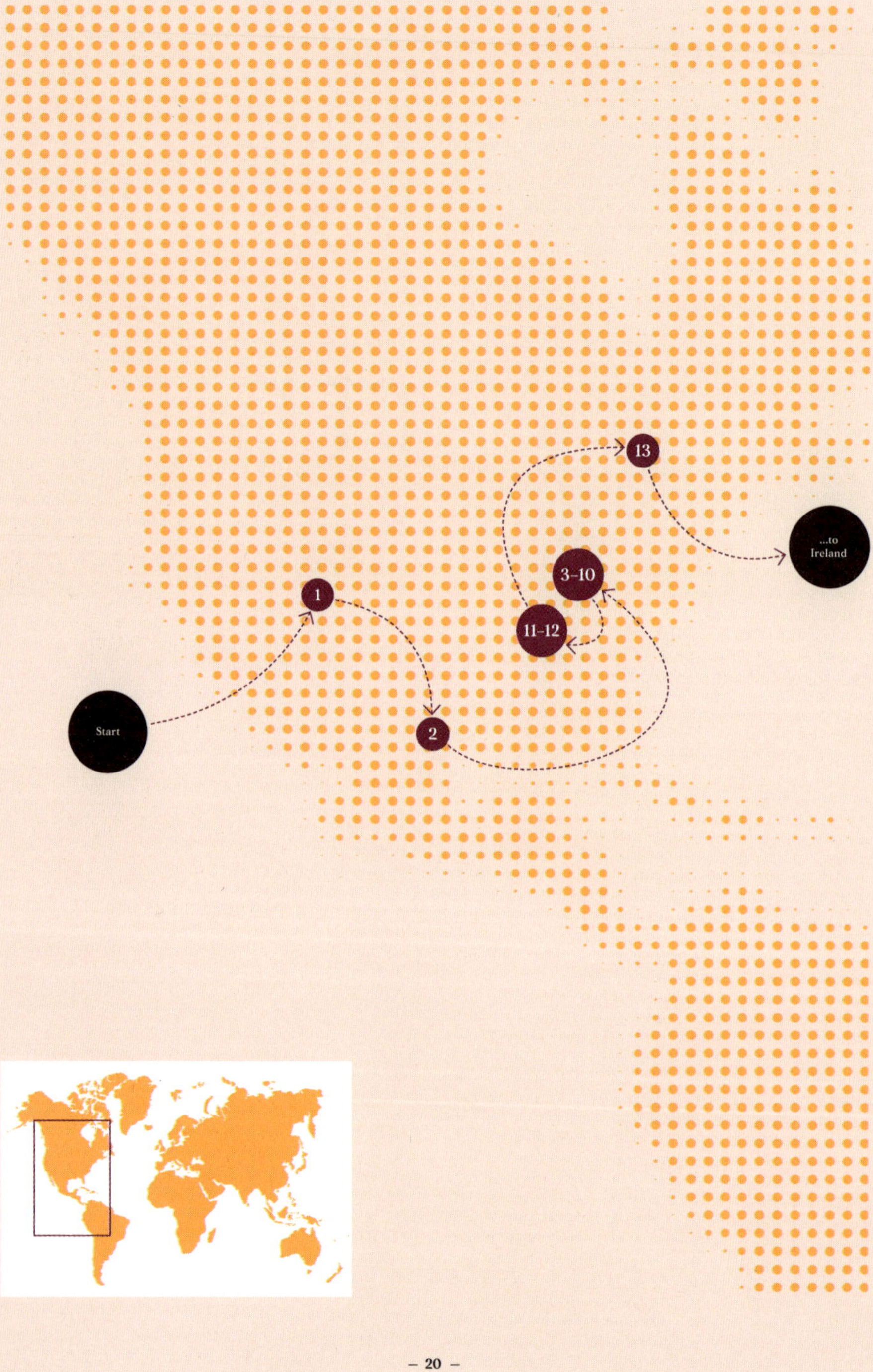

North America

A dispatch from North America

A brief history of North American whiskey

Whiskey has been a staple of rural American life for over two centuries, brought by European settlers. The Celtic-backed Scots, Welsh and Irish – already adept at distilling – honed their skills using local crops (corn, wheat and rye) and developed 'bourbon whiskey', America's native spirit.

Bourbon's heartland is Kentucky and just over the state's southern border lies Tennessee, which has its own unique whiskey-making process. Both styles have been exported around the world, and American whiskey is now renowned.

It is impossible to talk about the history of American whiskey without mentioning the Prohibition era, or 'the great experiment'. The Volstead Act was in place from January 1920 to December 1933, prohibiting the production, importation, transportation and sale of alcoholic beverages. The effect on bourbon distilling was devastating. Before the Act, there were 3,000 licensed whiskey distilleries reported in America. During Prohibition, only six were granted an extension to distil, producing for medicinal purposes only.

The result? Post-prohibition, new (or restarting) whiskey distillers moved away from traditional, inefficient copper pot stills, to more modern column stills. Compare whisky distilling in Kentucky to that of Scotland or Ireland, whose producers rely on copper pot stills today, and you'll notice the difference.

Further significant legislation was passed in 1936, stipulating that only brand new, charred barrels could be used for the maturation of bourbon. This means the barrels are highly active, and impart a full flavour very quickly. Beneficiaries of this law are other whisky-makers worldwide, who employ the once-used American oak barrels for long maturation of their single malts.

What makes the whiskey different?

Whiskey-making is now prevalent across North America, with all styles made and matured. In Canada, whisky is serious business but the style differs from American bourbon as it is permitted to be sweetened slightly. Canadian whisky is made from a mixture of different cereals which, unlike in bourbon, are fermented, distilled and matured separately. With traditional Canadian whisky, two distinct styles of spirits are produced: a lighter-base spirit and a 'flavouring' spirit. The latter is designed to carry more texture and structure.

Crucially in Canadian whisky, 9.09 per cent of the final product can be added flavouring, as long as it supports Canadian

whisky's characteristics. This is often fortified wines, sometimes bourbon whiskey or even Scotch.

Bourbon, which is made across the USA but most famously produced in Kentucky, is made from a mixed mash bill of different cereals, with a minimum of 51 per cent corn. The other grains which are typically used are wheat, rye and malted barley (in tiny proportions, to help kick start fermentation). Each bourbon brand will have its own unique mash bill and many styles can be made at one single distillery. As a general rule, most will use a corn, rye and malted barley mix. 'Wheated' whiskeys replace the rye with wheat.

After the spirit is produced, bourbon must be matured in brand new charred oak casks. However, there is no legal minimum length required. If a bottle of bourbon is labelled as 'straight', it will have spent a minimum of two years in new, charred oak casks. For 'bottled in bond', it must be at least four years old, bottled at 100 proof (50 per cent ABV) and be the product of a single distiller at a single distillery, in one season (January to June, or July to December).

Rye whiskey has seen a major uplift in popularity over the last decade, due to it being a prized ingredient in cocktails such as a Manhattan and Old Fashioned. It is legally a rye whiskey if the rye content is over 51 per cent. A similar rule is applied to 'corn whiskey', but this must be made with a minimum of 80 per cent corn, with no ageing required.

There is a growing appetite for US-made single malts and in 2024, the Tobacco Tax and Trade Bureau (TTB) produced its first legislation for 'American Single

Malt Whiskey'. This whiskey style must be made from 100 per cent malted barley, distilled entirely at one US-based distillery and aged in oak casks (maximum capacity 700 litres/150 gallons). 'Straight American Single Malt' must be matured for a minimum of two years. It must be produced at no more than 160 proof (80 per cent ABV), stored at a maximum of 125 proof (62.5 per cent ABV), and bottled at a minimum of 80 proof (40 per cent ABV). No additives, other than water, can be used.

Probably the most famous name in the world of whiskey is Jack Daniel, a Tennessee whiskey distiller (see page 66). Whiskey from this state undergoes a special step, the Lincoln County Process, which passes the spirit through maple charcoal (charcoal-making process pictured above) before maturation starts, or sits with charcoal in a vat for a short period of time. The aim is to 'mellow' the spirit ahead of maturation. Think of it as a preschool for whiskey.

When to visit the distilleries

There is a growing scene for single malt production in North America, meaning there has never been a greater variety of distilleries to explore for the curious visitor. However, the heartland of whiskey-making remains in Kentucky and Tennessee, two states that share a border but have different approaches to their whiskey-making.

There's never really a bad time to visit Kentucky and Tennessee as the states are magic all year round. But, if you're going to make the pilgrimage, you might as well do it right. The key distilleries are dotted on farmland across the two states and it will take some planning – and a car or a driver – to visit them all. Note that Kentucky state spans two time zones, so please double check the times for tours.

Some of the Kentucky distillers have a solution. Along Whiskey Row, a main street in Louisville, you'll find micro-distillery visitor's centres on the Urban Bourbon Trail. This route gives you a far more immersive experience than travelling all the way out to some of the bigger, more commercial sites. And yes, some of these places also include fully functioning distilleries too. You can read more about these later in the book.

If you are keen to visit some of the distilleries' actual sites, however, then look no further than the Kentucky Bourbon Trail. Established in 1999 by the Kentucky Distillers' Association, the trail takes in some of the most iconic distilleries in the world and their website, kybourbontrail.com, is an excellent resource of history, maps, places to stay and transportation.

If I had to pick one time of the year to visit this famed whiskey region, it would be September when the Kentucky Bourbon Festival is on and the weather is at its peak – warm but not too warm. The event is held annually in beautiful, historic Bardstown

and is a celebration of all things bourbon in the heart of the 'Bourbon Capital of the World'. Held outdoors, bourbon producers come together with their own stands to showcase their wares.

Started in 1992 as a local affair, it has grown into a multi-day festival featuring tastings, exclusive barrel releases, cocktail competitions and behind-the-scenes tours at some distilleries. Attendees can immerse themselves in bourbon culture, mingle with master distillers, and enjoy live music, local food and educational sessions.

Tennessee is home to the world's most visited whiskey distillery. Asked to guess at this and most would say 'Jack Daniel's' (see page 66), but in fact this title goes to the Ole Smoky distillery in Gatlinburg near Knoxville, far east of Nashville.

Now, The Holler distillery does indeed make whiskey, and their range features a Tennessee Straight Whiskey. However, it is more flavoured offerings (think cookie dough, strawberry lemonade, and pineapple) of 'whiskey' for which Ole Smoky is famed, and their distillery is much more of a flavour-driven fairground than it is a whiskey-distillery visit. It warrants a mention, but for me it would be like taking someone to a fast-food burger joint when they've asked for a high-end steak house.

Tennessee is home to two cracking distilleries (Jack Daniel's and Nearest Green), both of which are pretty close to Nashville, the perfect place to base yourself for trips to either. Driving to them is a must, so try and go with a party greater than one, so at least some of you can enjoy the facilities on offer, especially the world's longest whiskey bar at Nearest Green (see page 70).

Stranahan's

SOUTH KALAMATH ST · DENVER · COLORADO 80223 · USA

Visiting Stranahan's in Denver, Colorado, is an immersive experience that gives whiskey enthusiasts and casual visitors a chance to explore the heart of one of America's most respected craft distilleries.

Located south of downtown Denver, Stranahan's distillery is housed in an unassuming industrial building. Once you step inside, you're welcomed into a warm and inviting atmosphere where the passion for whiskey-making is palpable. Despite its newness (the distillery was founded in 2004), Stranahan's is decked out like an old-school Americana store and has an almost vintage feel to it.

The distillery itself is geared towards making single malt, the unique pot stills here are worth the trip alone and the wash still looks like a large, upside-down copper version of Thor's hammer. The necks include plates for increased reflux.

The tours at Stranahan's provide an in-depth look at the entire whiskey-making process, including a check-in on its casks which mature at high altitude in a dry environment. This leads to losses but unusually it's not of alcohol but water, at a rate of over 10 per cent a year. This means that the ABV of the maturing whiskey rises instead of falls. For bottling, Stranahan's uses water sourced from the pristine Rocky Mountain snowmelt, adding a distinctly local character to its spirit.

Tours culminate in the tasting room, where visitors get to sample several expressions of the whiskey. There is also a distillery shop, or General Store as it is called here, where you can purchase bottles of whiskey, clothing and even hand-labelled, single-barrel selections that are only available at the distillery. Finally, there is the cocktail lounge, where you can relax with an Old Fashioned or highly limited releases such as its Snowflake bottling, which are not available elsewhere.

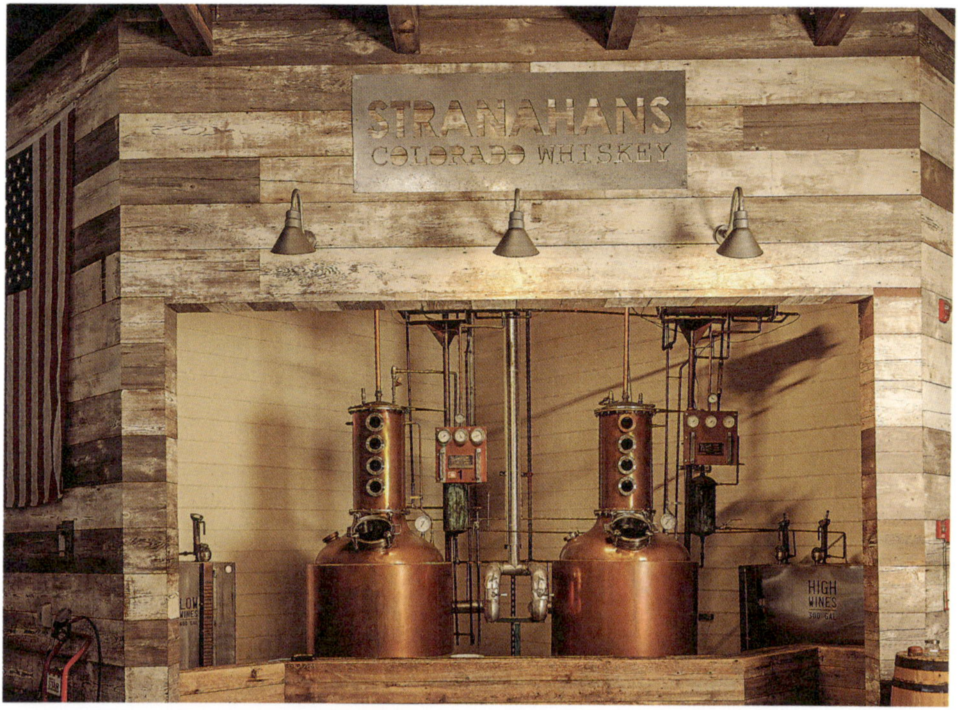
STRANAHANS
COLORADO WHISKEY
HIGH
WINES
300 GAL

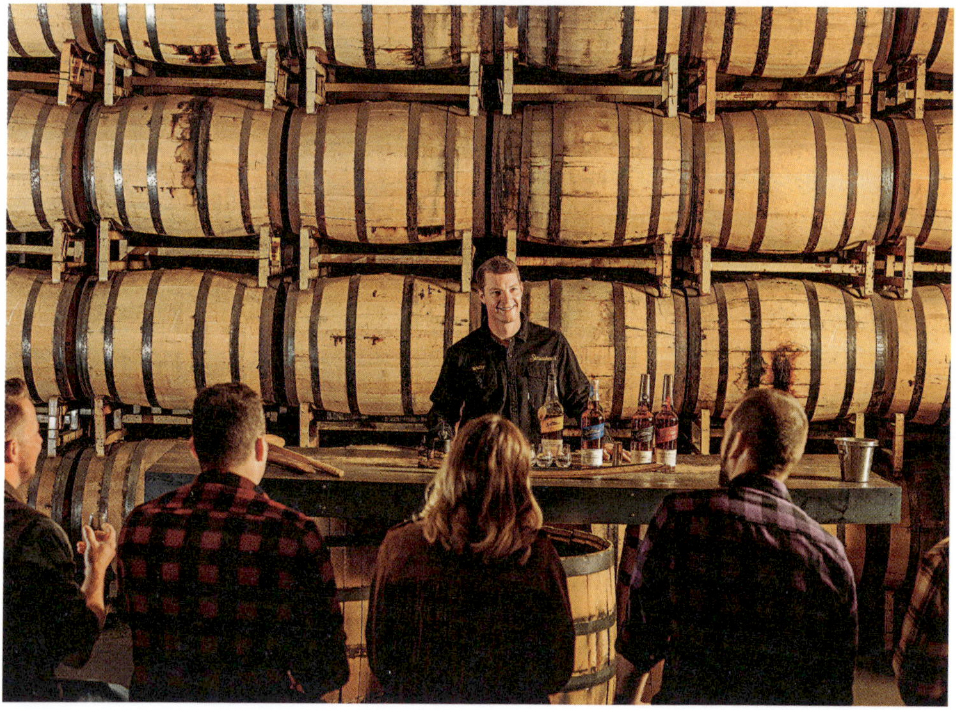

Origins

Stranahan's, known for its single malt whiskey, is Colorado's first legal distillery since Prohibition and has been pioneering American single malts since its founding in 2004.

The history of the distillery is rooted in a personal connection: George Stranahan, a local rancher and brewery owner, and firefighter Jess Graber (who met when Graber was attending a fire at Stranahan's farm) teamed up to create a uniquely Colorado whiskey. Their friendship and shared passion for spirits laid the foundation for Stranahan's.

Stranahan's Original

47% ABV

White chocolate and freeze dried raspberries on the nose, with an additional hint of pear drops and toasted almond flakes. The palate gives tonnes of melon, strawberries and heather, with some lavender sweetness. On the finish, spices of nutmeg and cinnamon are evident, all wrapped up in delicate oak vanilla.

Blue Peak

43% ABV

Toffee is the first aroma to rise from the glass, followed by plums and some red cherry notes. There is a big slab of vanilla with toasted pine nuts, too. The taste is underpinned with a sweetness of coffee, dark sugar, some light tea and a touch of honey on warm bread. The aftertaste gives orange, cloves, heather and more toffee.

2

Balcones

225 S. 11TH ST · WACO · TEXAS 76701 · USA

Not all American whiskey is made in Kentucky and Tennessee. In fact, there is a growing scene across the USA and one of the trailblazing distillers is Texan producer Balcones. The distillery is a testament to what can be done when you rip up the rule book and start again, and Balcones has come to define what 'Texan whisky' (note, no 'e') means.

You can't really miss Balcones distillery. Set in a former storage facility, the imposing building sports a water tower and almost Hollywood-esque sign that proclaims its name across the town of Waco, Texas.

This site has been home to Balcones since 2016 with a state-of-the-art distillery that has allowed for an increased production from its former site, as well as for a visitor's centre that enables tours to run. Despite the increase in size, the distillery team here wanted the copper pot still, made in Scotland, to retain the same dimensions as their old still, which had a lyne arm (see page 17) that crossed out of one building and into another. This meant designing an incredibly long lyne arm to fit into the new building, which wraps around the top of the still like a coil. This has resulted in a still house, and accompanying still, that is utterly unique.

Balcones is an ode to what you can achieve if you set out to do things differently, yet remain rooted in a sense of place. Its whiskies are big, bold and unashamedly Texan. Tours are regular and allow you to explore the distillation process, from grain to glass, and sample the distillery's innovative lineup of whiskies – many of which are released as limited editions.

Origins

Founded in 2008, Balcones quickly gained a reputation for producing innovative, high-quality American whiskey. It kicked-off life in a former welding shop in downtown Waco, under a freeway. It is the sort of place that feels part hipster, part skid row. It even built its own copper stills, although this was about fitting whiskey-making around what they had, not vice versa.

The team began with a simple mission: to craft original Texan spirits using traditional methods and local ingredients. But what does that mean? Making a whisky that is as big in flavour as a Texan ten-gallon hat, it turns out.

Balcones' flagship product, Texas Single Malt Whisky (one of the first single malt whiskies made in the United States) is a big, rich, complex and bold product made using Texan barley, and matured in new American oak barrels in some of the hottest warehouses I have ever been in.

In 2016, Balcones expanded to its new home in a former red brick Waco storage facility. The reception to Balcones and its trend-setting Texan whisky has been so great that in 2022 it was purchased by whisky-focused distilling giant, Diageo.

Balcones Texas 1 Single Malt

53% ABV

The nose offers strong toasted aromas of dark coffee, complemented by rich chocolate and cocoa. On the palate, it brings a warming sensation with flavours of toffee, toasted hazelnuts and a hint of pistachio. The finish is very dry, dominated by oak spice and subtle barbecue notes.

Balcones Baby Blue Corn

46% ABV

You'll notice scents such as cream soda, root beer, and ice-cream Coke float and a touch of fresh ginger. There's also a hint of hot buttered corn. The palate reveals a mix of manila envelope, hazelnuts, charred asparagus and toffee, with spiced orange tea lingering on the tongue.

3

Maker's Mark

3350 BURKES SPG RD · LORETTO · KENTUCKY 40037 · USA

Hidden away in the rolling hills of Loretto, Kentucky, is Star Hill Farm: the home of Maker's Mark whisky. The campus, set across 1,110 acres, is more than just a distillery. It is also a working farm, art gallery and museum all in one.

Approaching Maker's Mark distillery feels like arriving on the set of a Western. The scene, with its rolling green pastures and rustic charm, is more farmstead than factory; a bucolic haven devoted to the art of whisky-making. Star Hill Farm is a remarkable site that has woven sustainability into its very soul, offering a modern-day pilgrimage for lovers of craft and character.

Your introduction begins at the welcome centre where, beneath the glow of Dale Chihuly's exquisite glass sculptures, and other works by American artists which grace the walls, the scene is set for a day of engaging all your senses.

The real attraction here is the soft, wheat-forward whisky, known around the world not by the name of the farm, but by the title of 'Maker's Mark', and the distillery that produces this spirit. The main hub of the campus, where the distilling magic happens, has its own visual impact: a black wooden tower with red shutters reaches to the sky, its angular shape contrasts with the giant, round grain silo which holds the all-important red winter wheat on which this whisky has built its famously smooth profile.

Inside, tall stills gleam like ancient relics and the air is thick with the sweet, yeasty aroma of fermenting grains. The tour here is a sensory journey, starting with open-top wooden ferments bubbling away a concoction of 70 per cent corn, 16 per cent wheat and 14 per cent malted barley. After a run through the tall column stills, a portion of its whisky-spirit is matured uniquely in a cool cellar cut into a chalk hill (see: Cellar Aged, overleaf), which also forms part of the tour. The rest relaxes in warehouses scattered around the site. Tours culminate with just one of the many elements that separates Maker's Mark from the rest: the wax dipping line. Each and every bottle is individually hand-dipped in red wax – and you get the chance to do it yourself in the visitor's centre store. Another signature flourish for Maker's Mark is that each and every label applied is hand-cut. This is true craft in action: tradition embraced by modernity, simplicity elevated by craftsmanship.

Star Hill Farm and Maker's Mark is a model of mindful stewardship and has been accredited as a B-Corp producer. The site has implemented numerous eco-friendly practices, such as recycling waste materials and using renewable energy sources, and operates as a zero-landfill business; quite remarkable for such a huge, global brand. Additionally, the farm's land management practices are designed to preserve the natural beauty and health of the local ecosystem, and many of the ingredients served in their incredible onsite restaurant, as well in their fantastic cocktails, are raised or grown on the farm.

Star Hill Farm, driven by the whisky produced there, is almost a small whisky republic in its own right, and current Managing Director Rob Samuels could easily hold the tile of 'Governor of Star Hill

Farm' such is the independence and self sufficiency of this place. You visit Star Hill Farm for the whisky, but you stay for the art, the food, the cocktails, and ultimately the welcome.

Origins

The Samuels family, who founded Maker's Mark, didn't just make bourbon; they crafted a legacy. In 1953, Bill Samuels Sr. together with his wife, Margie, developed a whole new recipe with the aim of making a smoother, wheat-forward bourbon. What emerged was a whisky that defied convention, eschewing the usual rye for red winter wheat. This subtle change became Maker's Mark, which takes its name from Margie's collection of English pewter, famed for being stamped with the mark of each maker. Where Bill was responsible for the recipe of this revolutionary whisky, it was Margie who was left with the creative reins. She developed the signature bottle shape that is still used today, as well as the wax-dipped tops. The first bottles of Maker's Mark were sold in 1958 and they were instantly recognisable due to their distinctive packaging. The signature wax dip not only made Maker's Mark bottles stand out on the shelf but also emphasised the handcrafted nature of the product.

The Samuels family has been instrumental in the development of the distillery, and they still run the operations to this day. Bill Sr and Margie passed the distillery on to Bill Jr. Today, it is his son, Rob, who holds the title of Managing Director with Maker's now part of the multinational spirits company Suntory Global Spirits.

Maker's Mark Kentucky Straight Bourbon

45% ABC

The distillery's core product presents a delightful bouquet of caramel, vanilla and a hint of toasted oak. The palate holds a creamy texture with notes of toasted marshmallow, rich caramel and vanilla with a subtle nuttiness. The finish is long and satisfying, with lingering flavours of sweet vanilla, a touch of honey and a whisper of spice.

Maker's Mark Cellar Aged 2023

57.85% ABV

Sophisticated aromas of dark chocolate, dried fruits and deep oak are complemented by subtle hints of vanilla and tobacco. On the palate, it offers a luxurious mouthfeel with flavours of caramelized brown sugar and robust oakiness. The finish gives a long, lingering cinnamon spice.

Buffalo Trace

113 GREAT BUFFALO TRACE · FRANKFORT · KENTUCKY 40601 · USA

Of all Kentucky's distilleries, Buffalo Trace has gained a reputation for producing a number of highly sought after bourbon brands, including storied names such as Pappy Van Winkle and the Weller range. Visit to discover what makes the distillery's whiskeys so special.

You can't really miss the Buffalo Trace distillery. It is signposted by a huge, imposing water tower branded with the distillery's name and a giant image of a buffalo. This is a distillery that knows the value of its labels, and the attraction of high-quality whiskey.

Built alongside the Kentucky River in Frankfort, the campus is steeped in history. The first thing that strikes you upon arrival is the beauty of the setting. The distillery's sprawling grounds are dotted with traditional brick warehouses, white fences and lush greenery, which all set the stage for an unforgettable tour. Named after the ancient buffalo migration trails that once crisscrossed the region, the distillery's connection to the land feels immediate and authentic.

Buffalo Trace is home to some of the best loved and most sought after whiskeys in America. The legendary Pappy Van Winkle label is one of the star attractions, with many visitors asking if it is for sale in the onsite store. Occasionally, it is. More likely, though, you will find other beloved bourbons such as Weller, Blantons, George T Stagg or Eagle Rare, with barrel picks often available.

Times are good at Buffalo Trace and, in 2013, the distillery doubled its capacity. Today, it runs two primary styles of mash bill (No. 1 and No. 2). The details are undisclosed but it does say that No. 1 is a 'low rye' makeup while No. 2 is 'high rye'. It is its 'wheated mash bill' that the Pappy Van Winkle and Weller brands are built on. There are other mash bills in production on this complex campus, including rye-forward for Sazerac, for example, and there is a focus on experiments, too.

The distillery's tours are many and varied, including the Trace Tour, which gives a broad overview, and more specialized options such as the Hard Hat Tour, which dives deeper into the production process. Whichever you choose, expect an informative and engaging experience. Remarkably, all tours at Buffalo Trace – which include a tasting of its products – are complimentary, so pre-registration is advised.

Origins

The Buffalo Trace distillery is one of the oldest continuously operating distilleries in the United States, with a rich history dating from 1775. It wasn't until 1812 that a registered distillery was built by Harrison Blanton, the man whose name is found on the brand's bottles of whiskey.

The distillery has changed hands multiple times, to notable figures like Edmund H Taylor, the first man to give the distillery its name of Old Fire Copper (or OFC). In 1870, the distillery was purchased by George T Stagg. Under Stagg's leadership, the distillery expanded significantly, becoming one of the largest and most important producers of whiskey in the United States.

Despite the challenges of Prohibition, Buffalo Trace continued to operate legally,

producing medicinal whiskey. This period helped the distillery solidify its place as a resilient and essential part of American whiskey-making.

The distillery was officially renamed Buffalo Trace in 1999 and is now owned by the Sazerac company. One of the most desirable labels produced under the stewardship of Buffalo Trace is Pappy Van Winkle. Initially made at the Stitzel-Weller distillery, which closed in 1991, original bottlings included whiskey from this shuttered site.

Today, the whiskey in these bottles is produced at Buffalo Trace as a joint venture with the Old Rip Van Winkle distillery company, and it has a cult following. The late writer and chef Anthony Bourdain said about it in 2012, 'If God made bourbon, this is what he'd make'.

Eagle Rare
10 Years Old

45% ABV

Beautiful nose of old leather, vintage books and warm pine with some pipe tobacco. The palate has warming spices, a pine and oak mix and some rum and raisin chocolates. The finish is red apple wrapped in oak and dusted with delicate cinnamon sugar.

Buffalo Trace

40% ABV

This spirit has a subtle aroma of spiced mint tea, nutmeg and cinnamon, with some oak spice and black cherry. There is a rich and complex flavour of warm liquorice, fresh coffee and red maraschino cherries. The finish has some sweetness but more astringent and tannin notes of well brewed tea and oak with some toasted marshmallow.

5

Woodford Reserve

7785 MCCRACKEN PIKE · VERSAILLES · KENTUCKY 40383 · USA

While most Kentucky bourbon distillers use column stills (see page 17), few are focused on traditional copper pot stills. Woodford Reserve is one that is, and it has reignited this tradition at its stunning distillery.

Right in the heart of Kentucky whiskey production is a premium pot still producing American bourbon: Woodford Reserve. The distillery takes its name from its location, Woodford County, which lies just off Interstate 64 between Louisville and Lexington, and is just south of Frankfort.

The typical vision of an American bourbon distillery is one of a large campus with huge distillery buildings and even bigger warehouses, producing a range of labels from multiple mash bills. It is against this backdrop of large column distillation and multi-brand production facilities that makes the Labrot & Graham distillery, as it was formerly known, such a unique and, quite frankly, beautiful proposition.

When this small, farmstead-style shuttered site was recommissioned by owners Brown-Forman, three copper pot stills were commissioned from Forsyths of Scotland. This is unusual for the bourbon industry, which leans into the use of column stills. This provides something of a challenge when it comes to distilling its mixed mash bill of corn, rye, wheat and malted barley which, after brewing in the open-top vats, isn't filtered before triple pot still distillation.

Woodford Reserve's mash bill is key for its core product, the Distiller's Select, made up of 72 per cent corn, 18 per cent rye and 10 per cent malted barley. Its rye offering has 53 per cent rye, with 33 per cent corn and 14 per cent malted barley. Its wheated offering uses 53 per cent wheat, 20 per cent malt, 20 per cent corn and a hit of 8 per cent rye. Under the watchful eye of current master distiller Elizabeth McCall, more varieties and experiments are expected.

During distillation, the cut point is set at 77.5 per cent ABV (155 proof), well below the 160-proof legal cap on American bourbon whiskey 'new make'. Woodford also barrels at 55 per cent ABV (110 proof), coming in at 15 degrees below what is legally allowed in the region. All this makes for a soft, fruity bourbon. There is heated warehousing, as well as double matured whiskey for a range of different expressions.

The distillery has recently undergone a visitor's centre renovation, offering tours, tastings, cocktails and a bottle shop.

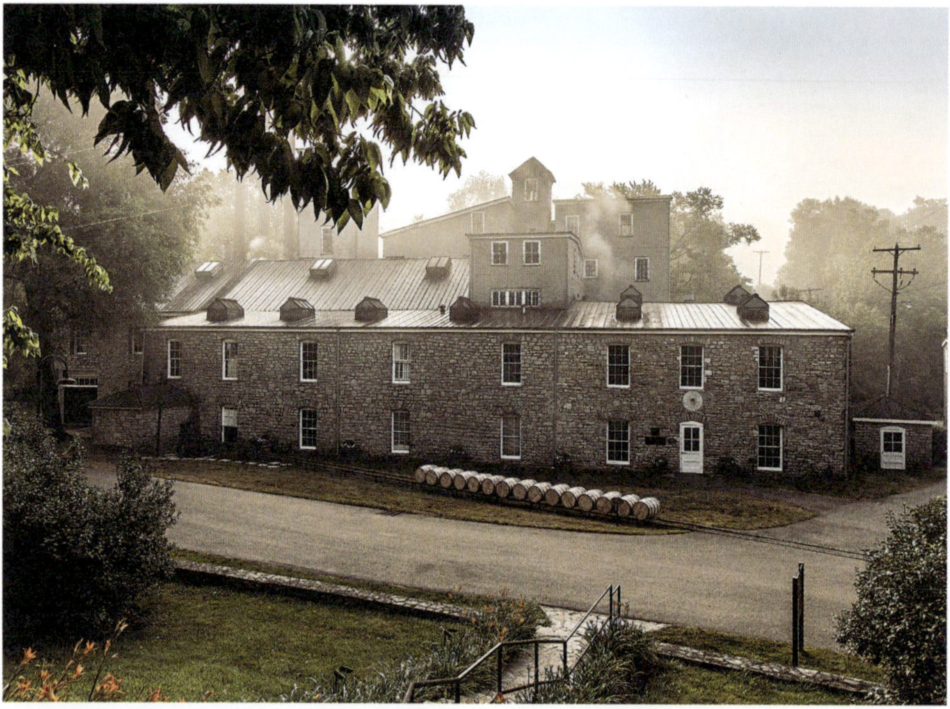

WOODFORD RESERVE DISTILLERY
96 J17
TENTH
ANNIVERSARY
1996
2006
DSP-KY-52

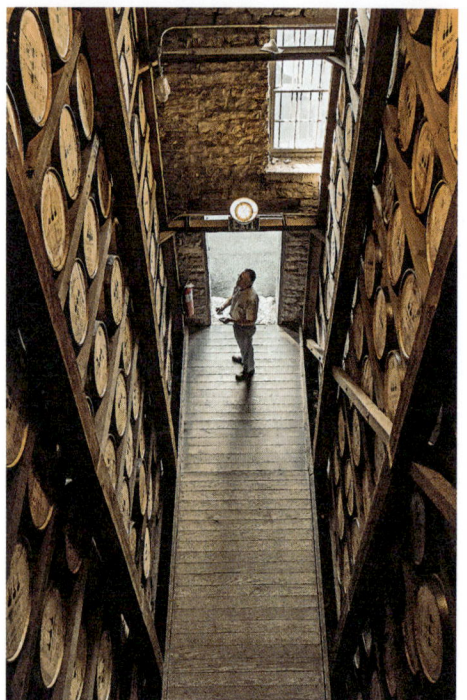

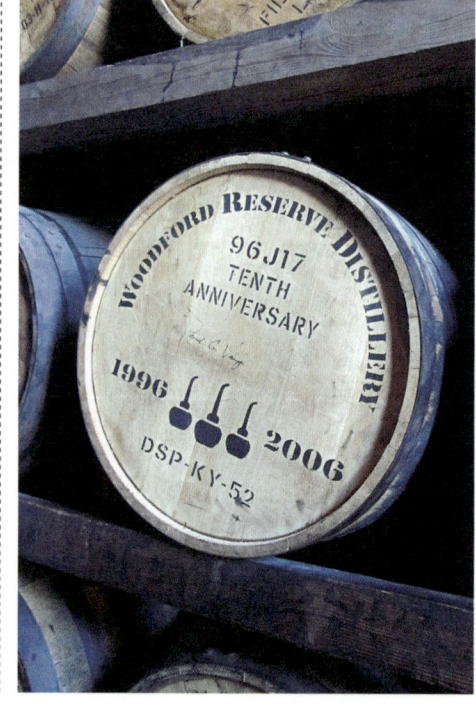

Origins

Labrot & Graham distillery, which is now known as Woodford Reserve, is one of the oldest and most historically significant sites in Kentucky. Located in Versailles, the site was initially founded as the Old Oscar Pepper distillery in 1812 by Elijah Pepper and was then run by his son, Oscar. It became home to Dr Chris Crow, the man credited with perfecting the sour mash method, the proof system (see page 18), the hydrometer and, some say, the concept of charring barrels before maturation. He was quite the inventor!

In 1878, the distillery was named the Labrot & Graham distillery after Leopold Labrot and James Graham of Labrot & Graham took over the site. The pair operated the distillery until 1941, when it was purchased by Jack Daniel's owner Brown-Forman. In 1968 Brown-Forman sold the distillery as farm buildings and it fell silent for a quarter of a century, until the former owners purchased it back from the farmer to whom they had originally sold it to. They restarted distilling on the site with production beginning in 1996 under its new name, Woodford Reserve.

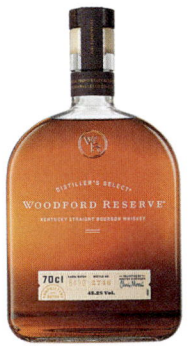

Woodford Reserve Distiller's Select

43.2% ABV

The Distiller's Select has notes of slightly damp wood, with nutmeg and warming allspice. The palate includes ginger cake, toasted marshmallows, runny honey and roasted peanuts. The finish gives more spice, candied ginger and some vanilla.

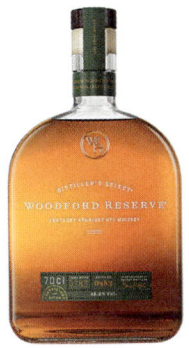

Woodford Reserve Rye

45.2% ABV

Expect a nose of toffee apple, pancakes, mānuka honey, royal jelly and fresh linen. The palate offers sweet honey, green apples and red grapes with candy cane and orange flower, and a finish of orange peel, cloves and cedar.

6

Rabbit Hole

711 E JEFFERSON ST · LOUISVILLE · KENTUCKY 40202 · USA

Rabbit Hole distillery sounds like something out of Lewis Carol's *Alice in Wonderland*, and indeed this is a place where whiskey moves in mysterious ways. Despite being a new player on the bourbon stage, its range is diverse and interesting, and incredibly drinkable.

From the outside, the distillery (which seems to take up an entire block in the East Market, or the NuLu neighbour of Louisville), is all modernist and angular, with large displays of art and some graffiti too.

It is really quite spectacular; the Rabbit Hole team call it the 'architectural icon of the Kentucky bourbon trail'. They're not wrong. This state-of-the-art facility might initially seem like a place focused on production but, on entering the distillery, you are greeted warmly by the team in a shop-cum-reception area that stocks whiskeys, of course, but also cigars aged in ex-whiskey barrels, books, glassware and clothing.

The whole distilling process is here to see, from open-top fermentation to the distillery's tall column still – all visible through glass walls that give you an up-close view of the spirit being crafted. Rabbit Hole embraces transparency, both literally and figuratively, in how it produces its bourbon; each step of the process, from the milling of grains to fermentation, distillation and ageing, is talked through in detail.

The distillery also features the Overlook Tasting Room, open until 4:30pm whenever the distillery is open. Tasting flights can be purchased, as well as cocktails, and you don't have to take a tour to visit the bar.

One of the most distinctive aspects of Rabbit Hole is its commitment to creating unique and bold bourbon expressions. Unlike many distilleries that rely on externally sourcing bourbon from other whiskey producers for their early releases, Rabbit Hole proudly distils all of its spirits onsite, save for some of their rarest limited editions. These whiskeys, from founder and whiskey maker Kaveh Zamanian's personal collection of casks, appear on a semi-regular basis under the Founder's Collection label.

Zamanian experiments with a variety of grains, ageing techniques and cask finishes, creating complex whiskies with distinct flavour profiles including Cavehill (a four-grain bourbon), Boxergrail (a rye whiskey), and Dareinger, which is finished in Pedro Ximénez sherry casks, adding a layer of rich, fruity complexity.

Origins

Rabbit Hole has a relatively recent yet impactful history in the world of bourbon; the distillery was founded by Kaveh Zamanian in 2012. He was inspired to create his own whiskey brand after moving to Kentucky and developing a deep appreciation for the spirit. His goal was to challenge the norms of the industry while keeping traditional production practices in place. The name 'Rabbit Hole' reflects his personal journey into the world of whiskey, symbolizing the idea of going down a path of discovery and risk. This theme of exploration is woven throughout the entire distillery experience at their location in the heart of Louisville.

In order to produce its whiskey entirely in-house, Rabbit Hole invested in a new, state-of-the-art distillery, which quickly became known for its distinctive architecture and cutting-edge technology. It's here that Rabbit Hole experiments with its spirit. The company creates unique whiskey expressions using high-quality, non-GMO grains and a variety of mash bills.

In 2019, a majority stake of the company was acquired by French firm Pernod Ricard, owners of the Chivas Regal and The Glenlivet whisky brands.

Rabbit Hole Boxergrail Straight Rye

47.5% ABV

Fresh orange peel dipped in chocolate sauce with hints of cloves. The palate of the Boxergrail is sweet but balanced with nice rye notes and a hint of spice that's backed with maple syrup. The finish gives vanilla and more orange notes.

Rabbit Hole Cavehill Straight Bourbon

47.5% ABV

The Cavehill offers bold notes of cherry jam and bacon bits on the nose, as well as figs, dates and dry oak with an earthy undertone. The palate has some sweetness to it, but also a dry oak note and hints of cinnamon. The glass is rounded off with nutmeg and allspice.

7

Jim Beam

568 HAPPY HOLLOW RD · CLERMONT · KENTUCKY 40110 · USA

One of the biggest names, not just in bourbon but in the world of whiskey, Jim Beam has been at the forefront of ensuring whiskey is a drink that's enjoyed around the globe. Its distillery home in Kentucky reflects this.

The Jim Beam distillery, hidden among the rolling hills of central Kentucky, offers a chance to witness the process behind one of the world's best-selling bourbons. It is also home to a host of other famous names, including Old Grand-Dad, Knob Creek, Basil Hayden, Booker's, Baker's and Old Overholt.

The first thing that catches your eye on arrival, aside from the huge sign spanning the width of the road declaring the name of the distillery, is the grand scale of it. Unlike some of the smaller, boutique distilleries in the state, Jim Beam's operation is massive and it's a testament to the brand's global reach. The visitor's centre is warm and inviting, designed in a style that mixes rustic charm with modern amenities. It perfectly reflects the balance between tradition and innovation that defines Jim Beam bourbon.

Tours here are many and varied, with ten options at the last count including concerts and supper clubs. On top of this, the distillery runs one-off events which regularly appear on their website and mailing list. The tours, depending on your choice, take in a variety of different sections of the distillery, and uncover elements of different brands such as Knob Creek or Jim Beam itself.

This distillery, across three sites, is Kentucky's largest producer and they have adapted well for visitors to their Clermont campus where, in 2021, they opened the brand new Fred B Noe distillery, which is home to both innovation and small batch releases. It is led by Fred Noe's son and eighth-generation Beam distiller, Freddie Noe. The site is powered by renewable energy and offers distillation sessions, seminars, blending lab classes and a tasting bar. It also features a state-of-the-art classroom which is overseen by the University of Kentucky's James B. Beam Institute for Kentucky Spirits. Quite the place!

At Jim Beam you will find the Kitchen Table restaurant, which serves hearty local fare, and it has a brilliant cocktail bar, too.

Origins

It all began in 1795 when Jacob Beam, a German immigrant, sold his first barrel of whiskey, known as 'Old Jake Beam Sour Mash', in Kentucky. Over the next few decades, the Beam family continued to refine their recipe, passing the art of distilling through generations. By the mid-1800s Jacob's grandson, David M Beam, expanded the operation to meet the growing demand for bourbon, moving the distillery to Nelson County near a railway line for better distribution.

During Prohibition, the distillery was closed but the family were determined to continue. After the repeal of Prohibition in 1933, James B Beam, who was also known as Jim, rebuilt the business from scratch and renamed the brand as Jim Beam Bourbon.

At the age of 70, Jim Beam personally oversaw the reconstruction of the distillery in Clermont, Kentucky, which remains its home today. Under the guidance of Jim's descendants, particularly Booker Noe, Jim Beam continued to innovate. Today, it is the world's best-selling bourbon. The Beam family's legacy is still evident, too: Jim's grandson Fred and great-grandson Freddie are both leading the distillery – and its whiskeys – forward today.

The Jim Beam distillery in Clermont, Kentucky, offers a rich experience that blends history, craftsmanship and a true sense of American heritage. As one of the most iconic names in the bourbon world, Jim Beam has a storied legacy that spans more than 225 years. It is even listed in the *Guinness Book of World Records* as the oldest distillery in Kentucky.

Today, its whiskey is built on a base of two different mash bills: a low rye (75 per cent corn, 13 per cent rye and 12 per cent malted barley), which covers most of the brands, including Jim Beam itself. A high rye (27 per cent) is used for Old Grand-Dad and Basil Hayden.

Jim Beam Double Oak

43% ABV

The lightness of the oak works with the spices in the mash bill to create an easy nosing and easy drinking whisky. The palate has hints of root beer, cherry cola, barbecue and freshly ground ginger powder. The finish is well spiced with more root beer notes and some cloves.

Jim Beam White Label

40% ABV

White Label's nose gives plenty of vanilla, which is underpinned by a forest of mature oak and eucalyptus trees. The palate has menthol and spiced oak with cloves, which move into cherry jam doughnuts on the finish. Spiced apple and vanilla cream also appear.

Bardstown Bourbon Company

1500 PARKWAY DR · BARDSTOWN · KENTUCKY 40004 · USA

It is said that you can observe the economic health of a city by the number of cranes dotting the skyline. The more building work happening, the better. The Bardstown Bourbon Company (BBC as it is better known) is evidence of the strength of Kentucky's distilling scene: it showcases a number of fantastic new bourbon brands and a wonderfully educational visitor experience, too.

Firstly, let's talk about Bardstown itself. No visit to Kentucky is complete without a trip to this historic town, which is seemingly soaked in whiskey. The second oldest town in Kentucky, Bardstown is home to the annual Kentucky Whisky Festival and is nicknamed the 'Bourbon Capital of the World'. In fact, there's no better place to build a distillery, which is exactly what the team behind BBC did in 2014.

On arrival, the stunning site screams 'brand new' – this is a place that has been constructed as a cathedral to bourbon production, designed to distil the very best whiskey across a range of styles, for a range of clients, as well as its own in-house label. The stunning architectural, glass-fronted building comes across as part university campus, part modern airport terminal. Inside, there is a dedicated visitor's centre with giant TV screens that show off the distilling process live, like a sports bar that's dedicated to whiskey-making – and the style isn't hidden, either. Everything is on display; here, you are invited to watch, listen and learn.

Visitors can take immersive tours, which provide a deep dive into the production process and showcase the distillery's high-tech equipment and innovative methods. The onsite Kitchen & Bar is another draw, offering a fine-dining experience paired with expertly crafted cocktails and bourbon flights, all set against the backdrop of the scenic Kentucky countryside.

In addition to its distillation prowess and state-of-the-art facilities, BBC is known for its modern maturation warehouses. This includes one with giant glass ends, which encourage the sun's warmth in and, in turn, aids the speed of the maturation. BBC's products are as impressive as the building they're made in. Its lineup includes a variety of expressions under the Bardstown Bourbon label, such as the Fusion Series, which blends younger and older bourbons, and its Discovery Series, which highlights rare, older bourbons. It has also worked

with other distilleries, such as India's Amrut (see page 204), on cask swaps for whiskey maturation.

And there's another element that sets BBC apart from many other distilleries: one of the company's hallmarks is its Collaborative Distilling Program. This initiative allows external brands to work with BBC to create custom whiskey products using the distillery's cutting-edge facilities. This unique approach has not only helped the firm scale quickly but it has also fostered a sense of community and creativity within the industry.

In just a few years, Bardstown Bourbon Company has established itself as a leader in the new wave of bourbon producers, and is very much worth visiting.

Origins

BBC is a new but rapidly rising star in the world of bourbon. Founded in 2014, the distillery has quickly distinguished itself for its modern approach to whiskey production and its pioneering spirit. Unashamedly, BBC has been set up to produce its own house style of bourbon, but also to operate as a 'white label' distiller for others.

The distillery was the brainchild of Peter Loftin, a businessman with a passion for bourbon, and a team of industry veterans. Together, they envisioned a company that would blend traditional bourbon-making practices with modern innovation, creating a distillery that not only produced high-quality bourbon but also served as a hub for experimentation and collaboration. The company's ethos of transparency and ideation is evident in every aspect of its operations, from production to its visitor experience. In a short amount of time, BBC has made a significant impact on the bourbon industry.

BBC Kentucky Straight Bourbon

43% ABV

BBC's straight bourbon has a lovely nose of sweet tea, with hints of oak, some cinnamon sugar and apple doughnuts. The palate gives red summer fruits and grape juice, with a hint of caramel and white sugar. The finish is slightly spiced yet smooth and mellow.

BBC x Amrut

55% ABV

The aroma opens with bold notes of coffee and rich cocoa, accompanied by the scent of well-aged oak and the character of polished antique furniture. On the palate, there's a dry quality, reflecting its time spent maturing in oak. This is balanced by subtle hints of grape and a delicate sweetness. The finish reveals nuances of black tea, rounding out the tasting experience with a refined complexity.

9

Old Forester

119 WEST MAIN ST · LOUISVILLE · KENTUCKY 40202 · USA

Old Forester is one of the best whiskey attractions around. Located on 'Whiskey Row' in the heart of Kentucky's Louisville, Old Forester's unassuming façade conceals an expansive space complete with distillery, visitor's centre, bar and retail space. And it offers visitors a truly remarkable experience, too.

Old Forester really is a landmark destination. The visitor's centre and distillery opened in June 2018 in a return to one of its original locations. It also marks the first time Old Forester has had its own dedicated distillery in over a century, with the building on Main Street restored perfectly to preserve its historic roots, while showcasing modern amenities. The storefront hides a complete distillery with fermentation tanks, a giant, gleaming copper column still, coopering, warehouse, lab, tasting rooms, bar and retail space. All behind a simple door on Louisville's Main Street.

The highlights are many but include the onsite cooperage, where barrels are assembled. Visitors can watch them being fired – literally burned on the inside, with flames flying towards the ceiling – to the specifications that give Old Forester whiskey its distinctive flavour. This place is truly remarkable. So much so that tours are booked out three months in advance, so it is necessary to book early in order to avoid disappointment.

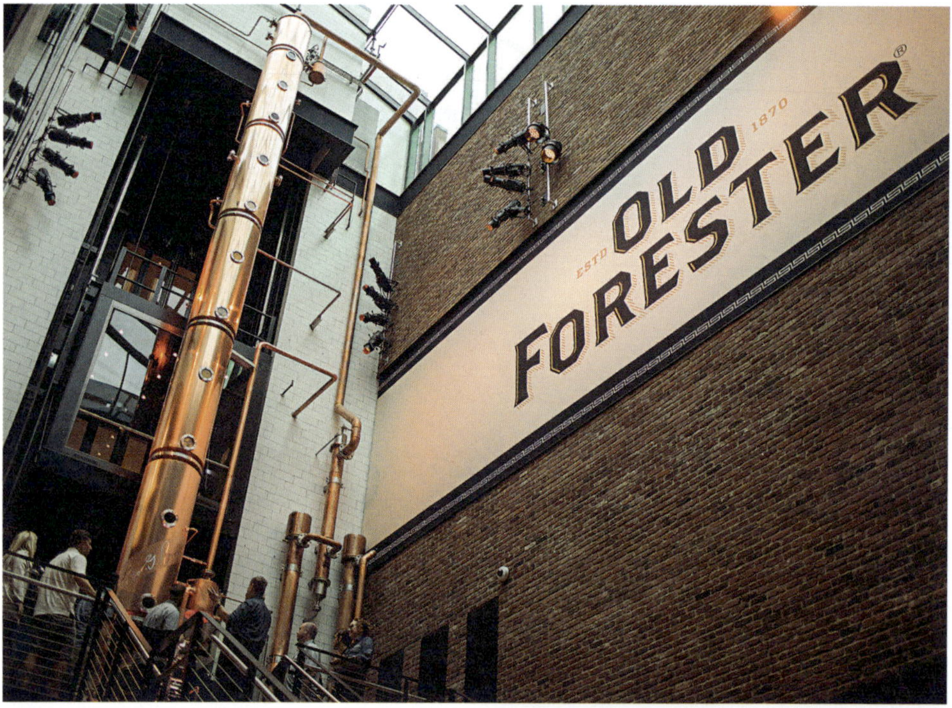
ESTD OLD 1870
FORESTER®

BOURBON WHISKY

HEAD IRON
HEAD HOOP

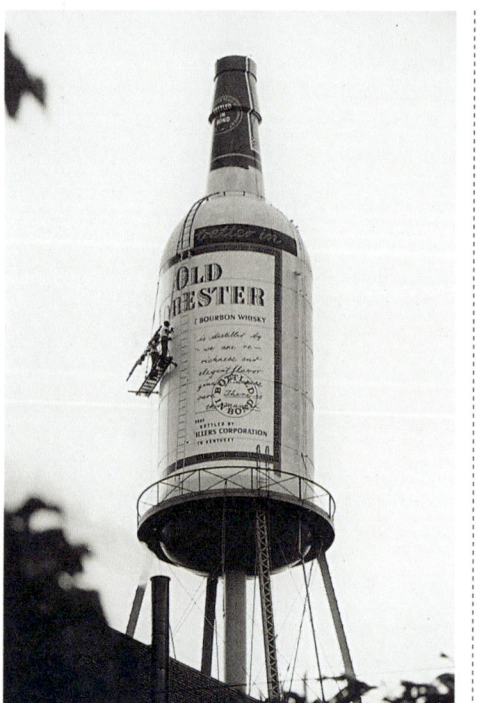

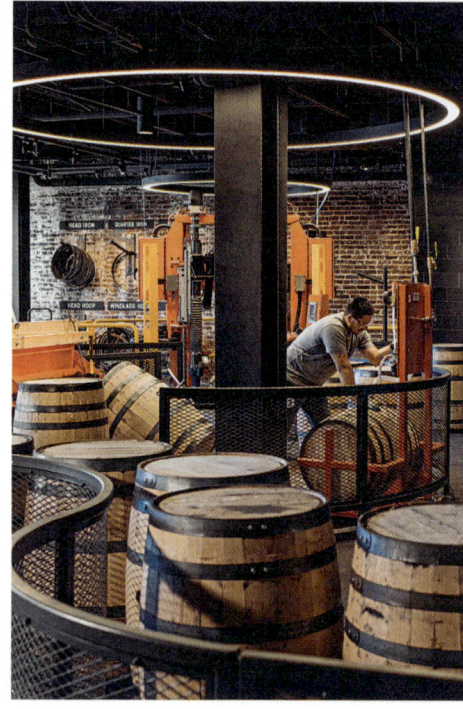

Origins

Old Forester, a classic American bourbon, holds a special place in whiskey history as one of the oldest continuously produced bourbon brands, dating back to 1870. It was founded by George Garvin Brown, a pharmaceutical salesman in Louisville, Kentucky, who sought to create a high-quality, consistent bourbon for medicinal purposes.

Brown was innovative in his approach and he became the first producer to sell his bourbon exclusively in sealed glass bottles, ensuring its quality and purity. This move marked Old Forester as one of the first bottled bourbons in the USA, a distinction that would become foundational to its reputation.

It was one of the few bourbon brands to be able to produce through the turbulent era of Prohibition, a time when most distilleries were forced to close, but Old Forester was granted a government approved licence for medicinal purposes. Today, the brand remains under the Brown-Forman Corporation (owners of Jack Daniel's, and Woodford Reserve) and is still family-owned.

Old Forester 1870

45% ABV

The nose is beautifully layered with intricate aromas of sandalwood, cedar, vanilla and maraschino cherry. On the palate, it unfolds softly, offering flavours of orange simmered with Cointreau, red apples and more cherry notes. The finish lingers with a touch of spiced cherry pie, adding a warm, satisfying conclusion to the experience.

Old Forester Kentucky Straight Bourbon

43% ABV

Impressively balanced, Old Forester's straight bourbon offers aromas of pancakes, crispy pancetta, savoury bacon and a touch of syrup. Those flavours continue on the palate, enriched by notes of allspice and cherry soda. The finish brings a hint of spiced cola, adding depth and complexity.

10

Wild Turkey

1417 VERSAILLES RD · LAWRENCEBURG · KENTUCKY 40342 · USA

Distilling whiskey is often about legacy. It could involve taking the work of previous generations and continuing with consistency, to keep the brand going in a new age. Or it could include innovation, pushing the whiskey forward for a different era of drinkers. Few distilleries have a legacy passed down through one single family; the Russells of Wild Turkey are a great example.

Arriving at the Wild Turkey distillery in Lawrenceburg, Kentucky, you might catch a glimpse of Jimmy Russell sitting quietly at the entrance, welcoming visitors to 'his' distillery. For someone like Jimmy, whiskey is not just about geography; it is about people. And for him, it's personal.

Jimmy has been at it for more than 70 years. Seven decades. Or just shy of a century. Since 1954 to be exact. That's a remarkably long time, by anyone's standards. His hands are the hands that built Wild Turkey's legacy, and he's passed that onto his son, Eddie, and his grandson, Bruce.

You could argue the mash bill of 75 per cent corn, 13 per cent rye and 12 per cent barley, or the 55 per cent barrelling strength, or simply the backdrop of the rolling hills of Kentucky and the charred oak barrels deserve the credit, but that's not entirely true. It's Jimmy's stubborn refusal to compromise and Eddie's willingness to push boundaries that make Wild Turkey what it is.

The Russells are the soul of this distillery, which is what makes it such an engaging place to visit. The whiskey is important at Wild Turkey, but not as important as the people there, be it the Russell family, or the visitors to the distillery themselves.

Tours at Wild Turkey revolve around a new architect-designed space that was completed in 2024, aptly named the Jimmy Russell Wild Turkey Experience. The 1,115-sq-m (12,000-sq-ft) space features a gift shop, intimate tasting room, bar and an outdoor deck offering views of the Kentucky River. An elevated lounge, called Generations, in a nod to the Russell family heritage, has stunning views over the valley atop of which the distillery sits.

Tours are available year round, but the distillery is closed on Mondays and Tuesdays. The trips include a History Walk, which takes you through a video corridor displaying the bourbon's history and evolution, elements of production and the Wild Turkey story itself.

Origins

In 1891, Thomas Ripy built the Old Hickory distillery in Tyrone, Kentucky, on the former site of the Old Moore distillery. One of the Ripy family's major customers was wholesaler and bottler, Austin Nichols.

The Wild Turkey brand is said to have been chosen as a name for a bourbon from this distillery after an Austin Nichols executive, Thomas McCarthy, took some on a trip hunting wild turkeys in 1940. From 1942, Austin Nichols began to label their stocks as 'Wild Turkey'. For the next 30 years, Austin Nichols remained a customer and, in 1971, purchased the facility, then known as the Boulevard distillery, changing the name to the Wild Turkey distillery.

The true red thread that runs through the distillery's whiskey production is the Russell family. Jimmy, his son and now grandson have been pivotal figures not just in the production of Wild Turkey but in the evolution of bourbon over the past half century. The Russells Reserve label was created by Eddie Russell, in honour of his father, Jimmy. Today, the company is owned by Campari, who purchased the brand from Pernod Ricard in 2008.

Wild Turkey 101

50.5% ABV

The nose is bold and robust, evoking the scent of weathered oak, freshly split after a rain shower. On the palate, rich oak continues to dominate, complemented by notes of blood orange, chopped hazelnuts and aged leather. The finish lingers with more blood orange and a subtle hint of mint, adding a refreshing touch to the complexity.

Russell's Reserve 10 Years Old

45% ABV

The nose is warm and inviting, with aromas of breakfast pancakes, waffles and a touch of leather, all accented by crispy streaky bacon lightly dusted with icing sugar. On the palate, you'll find iced tea, subtle ginger spice, and hints of cinnamon sticks. The finish is beautifully dry, leaving a refined and satisfying impression. Simply lovely.

11

Jack Daniel's

133 LYNCHBURG HWY · LYNCHBURG · TENNESSEE 37352 · USA

One way to discover a great whiskey experience is to look at new, interesting producers who are doing things differently. But that doesn't mean you should overlook the established players who have a long history of making great liquor. Jack Daniel's is a fine example. Its whiskey has been a constant on backbars – and home bars – for generations, and its visitor's experience shows off both its whiskey and history brilliantly.

The small town of Lynchburg, Tennessee, has been home to the Jack Daniel's distillery for more than 150 years. It welcomes a serious number of visitors each year and is set up with a good sized car park and lots of space around the main areas for relaxing. The distillery itself is situated in a picturesque rural setting, surrounded by wooded hills and the peaceful waters of Cave Spring Hollow, the natural limestone spring which has supplied the distillery with pure, iron-free water since the brand's very conception. Be under no illusion though; this is a big distillery with seven sets of stills and nearly two million barrels housed onsite.

There are several tour options available at Jack Daniel's, which cater to different levels of interest. The Distillery Tour is the most popular, offering a guided walk through the entire whiskey-making process. Visitors are shown each step in the process, from the milling of grains and fermentation in large, open vats to the distillation in tall column stills. The tour also highlights Jack Daniel's Lincoln County Process, where the whiskey is filtered through sugar maple charcoal, giving it the smooth finish Tennessee whiskey is known for. The traditional mash bill is 80 per cent corn, with 12 per cent malt and 8 per cent rye. There is also a 'high rye' option which kicks in at 70 per cent of the spicy cereal.

As you might expect from one of the world's best-selling whiskies, the tours at its distillery offer a deep dive into the history, craftsmanship and tradition behind the brand.

Tours end with a whiskey tasting experience in a beautifully designed tasting room. Visitors can sample various Jack Daniel's expressions before heading to the White Rabbit Bottle Shop. Moore County, where Jack Daniel's is located, is a dry county. So, how is there a bottle shop? The answer lies in the name: it sells the bottles, which just happen to be full of whiskey.

The town itself is almost an extension of the distillery, and the best place to eat is Miss Mary Bobo's Boarding House. Part of the Jack Daniel's family, it provides historic, collegiate-style dining rooms where groups of 15 eat local southern dishes family-style alongside the host's stories, who are mostly retired local ladies, about growing up in a town home to such a famous distillery. But there's no liquor with your lunch here, only iced tea.

Origins

It is impossible to talk about the worldwide success of whiskey as a drink without talking about Jack Daniel's. Along with Jameson from Ireland (see page 94) and Johnnie Walker from Scotland (see page 136) it is one of the first whiskeys that

people try. As such, there is a heavy burden on these brands to deliver the goods. Make a bad whiskey and you'll turn a customer off it for life. Make a good one, and you've got a new consumer base to grow. Today, it's not just about the liquid but the narratives that surround them, too. People don't just want a drink, they want a story in a glass. Jack Daniel's tells its tale well, and backs it up with a first-class spirit too.

The story begins with its founder, Jasper Newton 'Jack' Daniel who was born in 1849. In the 1850s, a young Jack was introduced to the world of distilling by Nearest Green (see page 70), an enslaved man who worked for Reverend Dan Call, a local preacher and distiller. Green, a master distiller, taught Jack his craft including the Lincoln County Process, where whiskey is filtered through sugar maple charcoal, which gives Tennessee whiskey its signature smoothness.

In 1866, at just 16 years old, Jack Daniel established his own distillery in Lynchburg near the Cave Spring Hollow. The distillery's flagship product, Old No.7, gained popularity for its unique smoothness and flavour, which was attributed to the charcoal filtering process. After Jack's death in 1911, the distillery passed to his nephew, Lem Motlow, who managed the distillery through Prohibition, World War II and the challenges of a changing industry. Today, Jack Daniel's is owned by the Kentucky-based Brown-Forman family.

Jack Daniel's Old No.7

40% ABV

The nose opens with a rich sweetness of vanilla, accompanied by hints of candy floss and toasted marshmallows. On the palate, those vanilla and marshmallow flavours deepen, carrying through to a finish where oak notes emerge and gradually take centre stage.

Jack Daniel's Gentleman Jack

40% ABV

Gentleman Jack presents aromas of allspice and fresh vanilla on the nose. The palate is rich and well-rounded, with deep notes of dark chocolate, cocoa powder and a touch of tropical fruit. The finish reveals a subtle oak spice and a hint of sweet black tea, adding a satisfying layer of complexity.

12

Nearest Green

3125 US-231 · SHELBYVILLE · TENNESSEE 37160 · USA

Nearest Green distillery's Uncle Nearest whiskey has exploded onto the spirit scene like very few brands before it. Looking to add to the canon of great Tennessee producers, the distillery is rooted in the story of the man who made it all happen in the first place, Nearest Green. The visitor's centre tells its exceptional story – that of an African-American female CEO giving long overdue credit to the previously enslaved master distiller – brilliantly.

Visiting Nearest Green distillery in Shelbyville, Tennessee, is a journey into a rich and often overlooked chapter of American whiskey history. Nearest Green honours the legacy of Nathan 'Nearest' Green, the formerly enslaved man who taught Jack Daniel the art of distilling.

Opened in 2017, the Nearest Green distillery is situated on a stunning manicured estate, a property that was previously home to an award-winning equestrian centre. Today, it hosts this thoroughbred whiskey distillery instead.

Visitors arrive in the vast welcome centre and shop. Tours happen on a regular basis and start with an engaging multimedia experience in what looks like a vintage chapel. In this fantastic room, you'll learn about Nearest Green and some of Tennessee's history in a video presented by Hollywood actor Jeffrey Wright. After the presentation, there is a comprehensive tour around the site and new distillery building, before a tasting and tour through a barrel house. The production here is classic Tennessee whiskey, with a column still and charcoal filtration.

After the tour, there is a chance to dine at Nearest Green's in-house restaurant, Barrel House BBQ, or take a drink at The Humble Baron cocktail bar, which features the world's longest whiskey bar – yes really – at 158m (518ft) long. It snakes around the giant warehouse-like building with a huge stage at one end, which opens up for outside performances. This distillery has it all, and is a place where you can easily spend an entire day.

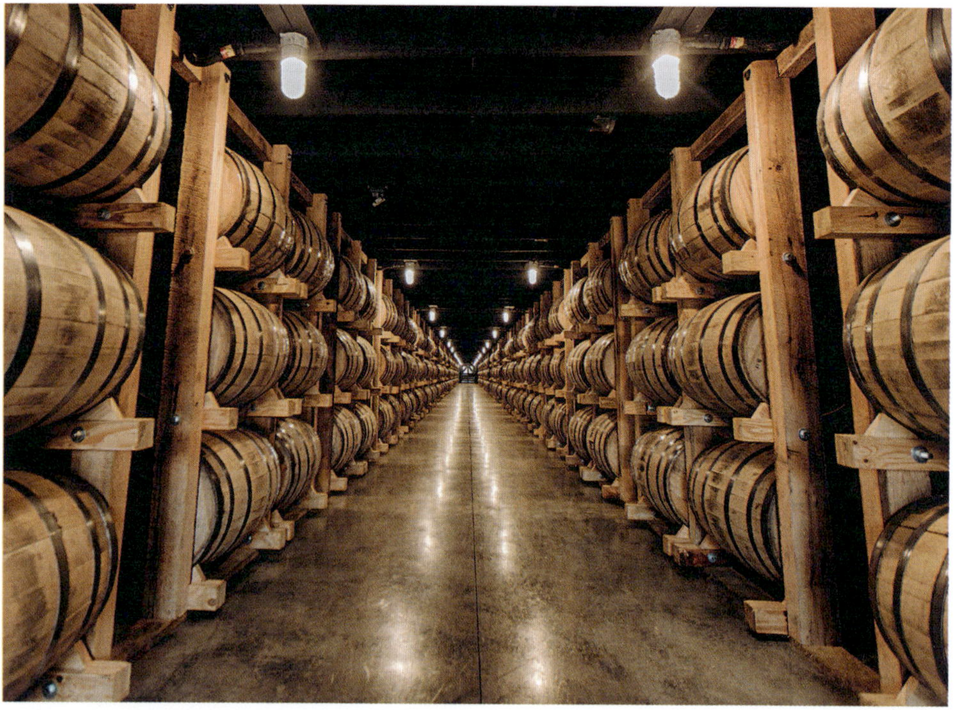

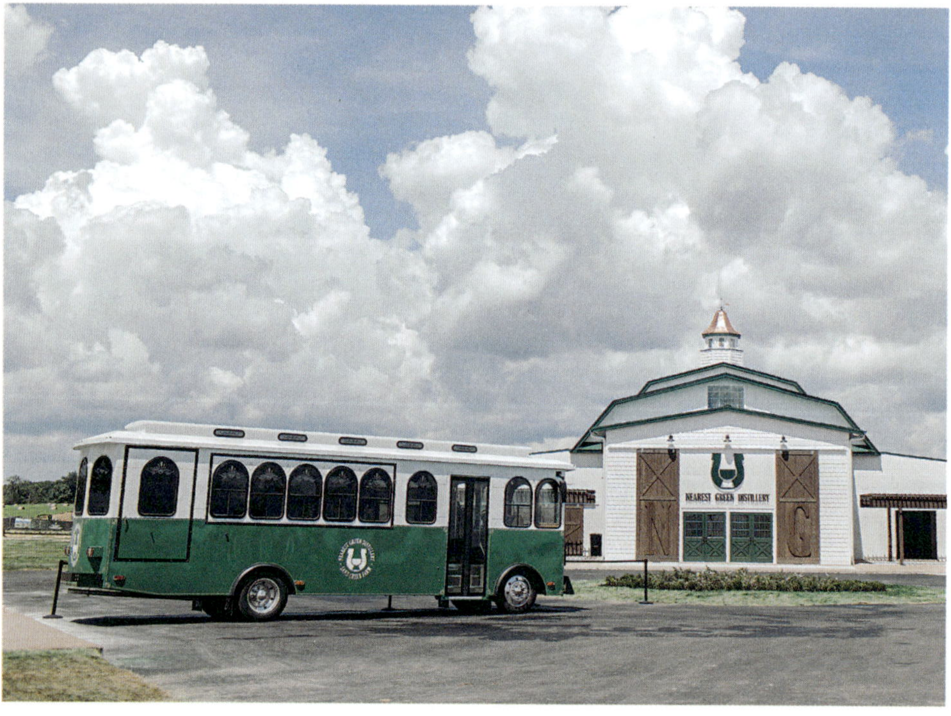
NEAREST GREEN DISTILLERY

Origins

To tell the story of Nearest Green is to tell a major, yet previously untold, story in the history of American whiskey. 'Uncle' Nathan 'Nearest' Green was an enslaved distiller of some repute in the local area, who ran the stills on a farm owned by Rev Dan Call. The reverend's whiskey was much admired due to a process that Green had developed: filtering the whiskey through charcoal for added smoothness.

It was on this farm where a young Jack Daniel met Nearest Green. Jack, a teenager at the time, was taken under the wing of Dan Call but it was Green who taught him the art of distilling. Green's expertise and mentorship had a profound impact on Jack, who later founded Jack Daniel's distillery and employed the newly emancipated Green as a master distiller.

In 2016, African-American entrepreneur Fawn Weaver discovered Nearest Green's legacy in an article about the distiller's influence on Tennessee whiskey making, written by bourbon expert Clay Risen in *The New York Times*. It inspired Weaver to seek out the story and shine a long-overdue light on Green. She conceived the idea for the Nearest Green distillery in 2017 to honour Green's contributions and legacy. The distillery opened in 2019 with Nearest Green's great-great-granddaughter, Victoria Eady Butler, employed as its master blender.

Uncle Nearest 1856

50% ABV

The nose is deep and rich, blending notes of rum with earthy, malty undertones. The palate is indulgent, offering hints of crème brûlée and red apples, leading to a finish of spiced custard tarts and subtle basil notes. It is rich and utterly delicious.

Uncle Nearest 1884

46.5% ABV

Crisp notes of freshly pressed apple juice are complemented by cracked black pepper and cocoa nibs. On the palate, a prominent grape-forward flavour is accented by cinnamon and allspice. The finish brings all these elements together, along with a touch of red summer fruits for added brightness.

13

Forty Creek

297 S SERVICE RD · GRIMSBY · ONTARIO · L3M 1Y6 · CANADA

Canada is home to a host of large whisky brands and distilleries that could offer fantastic visitor experiences. Sadly, few accept visitors these days, which is what makes a trip to the Forty Creek distillery, based in Grimsby, Ontario, so very special and unique.

A visit to the Forty Creek distillery provides a first-hand look at the craftsmanship behind the brand, which has been heavily invested in by owners Gruppo Campari (which has experience with both Kentucky's Wild Turkey – see page 62 – and Scotland's Glen Grant – see page 160 – on what a good visitor experience looks like). The Italian group purchased the distillery in 2014 and Forty Creek has since doubled in size. Located in the heart of Ontario's Niagara Peninsula, an hour's drive from Toronto, the surrounding region is known for its wine and stunning landscapes. Could it get any better? Let me tell you: the tours are free!

Each distillery tour begins with an introduction to the history of Canadian whisky, as well as Forty Creek's unique approach to production. Visitors are guided through the distillation process, starting with local grains. The use of high-quality corn, rye and barley from Ontario's fertile farmlands is key to the distillery's whisky-making process, as well as an explanation of the characteristics of each grain and what

they bring to the end product. The tour also provides a behind-the-scenes look at the cooperage, where visitors can see the barrels being toasted and charred.

One of the aspects that sets Forty Creek apart from other Canadian whisky producers is its constant drive for innovation. Throughout the distillery tour, visitors learn about the various experimental whiskies that Forty Creek has produced over the years, many of which are only available in limited quantities.

Forty Creek distils three mixed mash bills of grain separately, made up of rye, corn and barley. Each is distilled (in either column or pot stills), aged and then carefully blended, allowing for greater control over the flavour profile. Forty Creek's first major release, Forty Creek Barrel Select, was launched in 2000 and immediately garnered praise for its smooth yet complex profile. Since then, the distillery has introduced a variety of expressions, including limited-edition releases which have pushed the boundaries of Canadian whisky.

Origins

Forty Creek is one of Canada's most celebrated whisky producers, known for its innovative approach to traditional whisky-making methods. Formerly the eau-de-vie (grape brandy) producing Rieder distillery, the site was purchased in 1992 by winemaker John K. Hall who turned it into Kittling Ridge winery (which is still in operation today) before developing the Forty Creek whisky distillery. Since its launch in 1999, Forty Creek has become a major player in the Canadian whisky scene.

The distillery is renowned for creating rich, complex whiskies that blend craftsmanship, creativity and a deep respect for tradition. A visit to the Forty Creek distillery offers a deep dive into Canadian whisky culture, history and the art of whisky-making, while providing a sensory journey through some of the finest whiskies the country has to offer.

Established with an aim to breathe new life into Canadian whisky, a category that had long been dominated by a few large producers, Forty Creek draws on Hall's background in winemaking, bringing a fresh perspective to the country's spirit. His knowledge of fermentation, barrel ageing and blending from his wine-making days led Hall to experiment with techniques that took a different look at whisky-making.

Today, Forty Creek labels its bottles as 'Niagara Whisky' as a point of difference and, in 2020, Forty Creek was named Whisky Maker of the Decade at the Canadian Whisky Awards for its reputation of changing the country's whisky game.

Forty Creek Barrel Select

40% ABV

The nose offers a harmonious blend of green and red apples, leading into a palate that showcases a bright grape note alongside crisp apple juice and a hint of cider. The finish starts with a touch of sweetness before transitioning to a dry, lingering close. A beautifully balanced whisky from start to finish.

Forty Creek Double Barrel

40% ABV

With an Armagnac-like character, this whisky's nose features intertwining notes of vanilla and grain, complemented by a strong spirit presence. On the palate, ginger, spiced apple and red fruits emerge. The finish is delightful, featuring vanilla custard and warm apple pie, creating a comforting and satisfying conclusion.

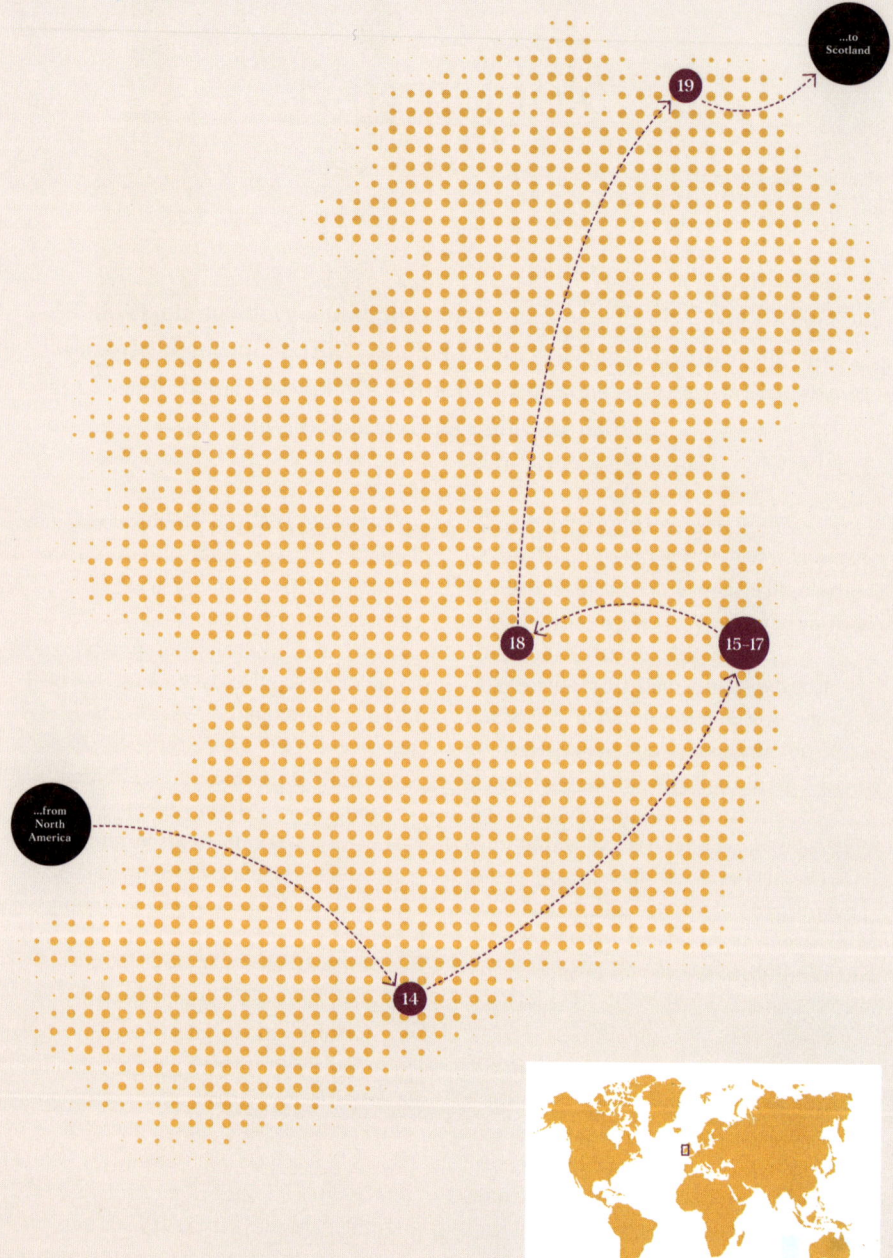

PART TWO

Ireland

A dispatch from the island of Ireland

A brief history of Irish whiskey

The story of Irish whiskey is one of remarkable resilience. At the turn of the 20th century, Ireland was a dominant force in global whiskey production with a massive output. In fact, one in every seven gallons of whiskey produced across the British Isles came from Dublin alone. Dublin whiskey was world-renowned and documents from the late 1800s note that the demand was more than five times that of Scotch.

A series of global crises – including the Great Depression, Prohibition, both World Wars, Ireland's 1916 Easter Rising and subsequent civil war, as well as pandemics – combined with overproduction and surplus,

delivered devastating blows to Ireland's whiskey industry.

By 1960, the number of distilleries in Ireland (now separated into Northern Ireland, a part of the UK, and the Republic of Ireland) had dwindled from 30 to just four: Bushmills in Northern Ireland, and Jameson, Powers and Cork Distilleries Company in the Republic of Ireland. In 1966, the latter three merged to form Irish Distillers, consolidating production at a new facility in Midleton, County Cork, leaving only two major producers on the island: Midleton and Bushmills.

It wasn't until 1989 when John Teeling converted an industrial distillery into a craft whiskey site, the Cooley distillery, that the green shoots of revival were seen. In 2010, Dingle distillery opened in the far western tip of the island. Now, the ball was well and truly rolling. It then took nearly 40 years for whiskey distilling to return to Dublin with the 2015 opening of the Teeling distillery (see page 86). Today, Ireland boasts more than 40 whiskey distilleries producing a wide range of styles, and the whiskey-world is a better, and richer, place for it.

What makes the whiskey different?

Irish whiskey comes in many forms but there is one style that is claimed as the island's own: single pot still. Designed as a pivot to taxation imposed on malted barley in Ireland in 1682 by the British Crown, pot still Irish whiskey uses a base of both malted and unmalted barley and is produced in exceptionally large copper pot stills. At the Midleton distillery in County Cork, home to some of Ireland's most famous brands, including Jameson and Redbreast, a ratio of 20 per cent malted barley, to 80 per cent unmalted barley is employed. The whiskey is then triple distilled and aged for a minimum of three years in wood.

Single malt is also made across the island of Ireland, with Bushmills the most famous example. On the whole, Irish single malt is made in almost exactly the same way as Scottish single malt but, like pot still whiskey, it also tends to be triple distilled. Across both single malts and single pot still, the Irish style is unpeated (save for a small amount of whiskey made at select distilleries) and celebrated for its smoothness and easy drinking profile.

When to visit the island of Ireland

Despite the growing whiskey scene across Ireland, much like Japan, there are no organized trails or whiskey festivals of note. The weather can vary wildly, even from day to day so, as such, there is no specific season

that is better or worse for a trip to Ireland. Thankfully, the resurgence of whiskey-making in Dublin has allowed more urban visitor's centres to open, meaning easier access to some of the newer producers such as Teeling or Roe & Co. The Jameson distillery in Dublin is a fantastic ode to the scene, and a decent redevelopment means it is modern, accessible and interesting.

If you are looking to get out and about to explore, Bushmills on Northern Ireland's coast is well set up for visitors and the surrounding area is used to tourists with the Giant's Causeway nearby. In the Republic of Ireland, the Midleton distillery is a short train ride from Cork, Ireland's second city, and has also been recently renovated.

14

Midleton

DISTILLERY WALK · MIDLETON · CO. CORK · P25 Y394 · REPUBLIC OF IRELAND

One of just two whiskey distilleries left in the Emerald Isle in the second half of the 20th century, the Midleton distillery in County Cork is the place to learn about Irish single pot still whiskey.

There is real history at the Midleton distillery in County Cork, Republic of Ireland. If it wasn't for this place, and Bushmills in Northern Ireland (see page 102), Irish whiskey distilling would have died out in the mid-20th century. In that regard, we have a lot to thank it for.

Despite being a short train or car drive from Ireland's second city, Cork, the quiet town of Midleton is not the obvious place to emerge as the saviour of whiskey-making in the Irish republic. Tucked away on the town's outskirts lies the distillery, a stately complex of stone and brick, glass and metal. Here, the ancient sits comfortably next to the modern.

This contrast has been driven by the huge growth in Irish whiskey sales over the last decade, particularly the Jameson brand, which has established itself as one of the best selling whiskeys in the world. In 1998, Jameson was selling around half a million cases a year (around six million bottles). In 2024, it sold 20 times that. This success has allowed Jameson's owner, Irish Distillers, to liberate some of the whiskeys in its portfolio which go into the Jameson blend.

The result? A relaunch of some of the historic brands that made Irish whiskey a powerhouse in the 1800s and early-1900s (see page 80), such as Redbreast, Green Spot and Powers, all of which are made at Midleton. And it wasn't just a relaunch of these brands, but a total revamp, with a focus on extending ranges, too.

As such, the focus on the Irish whiskeys made at Midleton has been sharper than ever. Today, Midleton is not just home to heritage brands, but forward-thinking Method and Madness, too. This label is rooted in a small, experimental distillery that sits within the old site as a new 'craft' (aka small) facility where younger members of staff – led by the masters who have been making whiskey for years – cut their teeth. The range covers experiments in the mash bill (oats, anyone?) and maturation (hands up for a mulberry cask matured whiskey).

The visitor's centre is brand new, having reopened in 2024 after a substantial renovation. There are six tours on offer, including the full-day Irish Whiskey Academy, which includes a deep dive into

whiskey production, from grain to glass, as well as cask sampling, too. The whiskey here is made in large copper pot stills, and the distillery has been expanded over the last few years to cope with the demand for Jameson – and the growing love for the single pot still whiskey brands.

Origins

The history of Midleton is the core chapter in the history of Irish whiskey, and the context of this can be seen on page 80 where there is a wider look at the turbulent journey this particular country has been on, as well as its whisky-making timeline.

Founded in 1825 by the Murphy family, the Midleton distillery quickly grew to become one of the largest and most important whiskey-producing sites in Ireland. It was

built near the Dungourney river, an essential water source for whiskey production. The distillery expanded throughout the 19th century, adopting new technologies and increasing its production capacity.

By the mid-20th century, the Irish whiskey industry was in decline. In response, several distilleries, including Midleton, joined forces in 1966 to form Irish Distillers Ltd. This merger aimed to consolidate resources and preserve the future of Irish whiskey. As part of this restructuring, production moved to a new, state-of-the-art facility built next to the old Midleton site, in 1975. The New Midleton distillery became the main production site for Irish Distillers' brands, including the iconic Jameson, Powers and Redbreast whiskeys.

Today, the New Midleton distillery is the largest in Ireland and has played a crucial role in the revival of Irish whiskey on the global stage. Under the ownership of Pernod Ricard, which acquired Irish Distillers in 1988, Midleton has continued to expand, producing some of the finest and most respected Irish whiskeys.

Redbreast 12

40% ABV

The aroma features griddled pineapple mingled with oak shavings and hints of vanilla pods. On the palate, you'll find a delightful combination of heather honey, red berries, banana bread and sweet toffee. The finish reveals flavours reminiscent of upside-down pineapple cake, creating a wonderfully nostalgic experience.

Green Spot

40% ABV

The nose presents enticing aromas of toasted almonds, hazelnut, the caramelized top of a crème brûlée and blackberry leaves. On the palate, you'll discover flavours of ginger cake, mint, thyme and basil. The finish is rounded and long, featuring grape-like notes that add a delightful complexity.

15

Teeling

13–17 NEWMARKET · THE LIBERTIES · DUBLIN 8 · D08 KD91 · REPUBLIC OF IRELAND

Few families can say they've had a systemic impact on a single whiskey scene, but the Teelings are one. Their distillery in Dublin was the first to open in the city for more than 125 years and their commitment to sourcing, selecting and bottling Irish whiskey under their own label refocused a world of whiskey drinkers back on to aged Irish single malt.

Unlike many other whiskey experiences in Ireland, which are often housed in historic buildings, the Teeling distillery is a fully operational facility in a purposeful, renovated structure. From the moment you step inside, you know you are about to witness whiskey-making in real-time. The distillery is located in the historic Liberties district, an area once known as the 'Golden Triangle' for its flourishing distilleries and, today, it's a hotbed of distilling once again.

Teeling tours offer an introduction to Irish whiskey, an exploration of the distillery itself and tastings. There is also a bottle-your-own option, too. The distillery triple distils in copper pot stills, as per tradition, but it also experiments with non-conventional cask-ageing, including rum and wine barrels. The distillery makes both single malt and single pot still (see page 81) spirits, as well as peated and unpeated whiskies.

Perhaps the most engaging aspect of the visit is the tasting session. Unlike many distilleries that focus solely on their flagship product, Teeling's tasting includes a selection of its various expressions, highlighting its diversity in flavour profiles. This includes its single malt, small batch blend and its grain whiskey. The tasting gives a good insight into the different styles of whiskey made across Ireland.

Teeling also boasts the stylish Bang Bang Bar, a whiskey-focused space that feels more like a trendy cocktail bar than a traditional tasting room. Here, you can enjoy whiskey cocktails – or sample more of the Teeling range – and it even has a terrace that overlooks the local area.

Origins

The Teeling family can trace their whiskey roots back to 1782, when Walter Teeling established a small distillery on Marrowbone Lane in the heart of Dublin, when the city was bustling with distilleries and Dublin Whiskey was a sought-after style in its own right.

Walter's original distillery was the victim of tough economic times, as well as political and social unrest, in Ireland and eventually all whiskey distilling disappeared from Dublin. The Teeling name resurfaced through pioneer John Teeling, a descendant of Walter. John established the Cooley distillery in 1987, helping to revive Irish whiskey distilling. The Cooley distillery was sold to Beam Global Spirit in 2011, and John went on to start The Great Northern distillery in Dundalk.

John's sons, Jack and Stephen Teeling, carried on the family tradition by founding the modern Teeling Whiskey Company in 2011. They initially sourced and bottled aged stocks from across Ireland (Cooley, of course), including 30- and 40-year-old Irish single malts (only one distillery could supply well-aged single malt at that point),

and won multiple awards along the way. It was in 2015, however, that they opened their own distillery, the Teeling Whiskey Distillery, the first new site in Dublin in over 125 years. This marked a significant milestone in the country's whiskey renaissance. In 2017, rum-giant Bacardi bought a stake in the business, increasing their ownership in 2024.

The Teeling Whiskey Distillery is a remarkable place for the simple fact that it is responsible for bringing whiskey distilling back to the city of Dublin, a place infamous for drinking, parties, hospitality and warmth, which was left dry of distilling from 1976 through to 2015. The return, by Teeling, of whiskey distilling to Dublin feels like the city's own pulse is quickening again, and key to this new heartbeat is the Teeling family's distillery.

Teeling Small Batch

46% ABV

The tasting begins with fresh, clear apple juice, complemented by hints of gorse and pear. It's light and delicate, yet there's a touch of wood spice in the background. On the palate, the texture is smooth, highlighting lighter toasted notes, where the spirit and oak harmoniously blend. The finish is driven by leather and citrus, with additional layers of tropical fruits, creating a beautifully balanced experience.

Teeling Single Grain

46% ABV

The aroma features custard Danish pastry topped with vibrant orange zest, along with notes of blood orange and cardamom. On the palate, it reveals rich, ripe fruits with hints of mandarin, cinnamon, syrup and mānuka honey. The finish is smooth and showcases elements of fennel and additional honey, which dominate the character of this whiskey beautifully.

16

Roe & Co

92 JAMES ST · THE LIBERTIES · DUBLIN 8 · D08 YYW9 · REPUBLIC OF IRELAND

Roe & Co is one of the most historic names in Irish whiskey and has been revived in recent years. Housed in the site of the old Guinness power station, and adjust to the Guinness Storehouse visitor experience, it offers a fantastic counterpoint for the pints on offer next door.

From the moment you walk through the doors at Roe & Co, the atmosphere is welcoming and vibrant, echoing the idea that Irish whiskey is fun and approachable. The distillery offers a multi-sensory experience that immerses visitors in the world of whiskey-making, from grain to glass. The journey begins with a deep dive into the history of George Roe, the man behind Roe & Co, whose whiskey empire in the 19th century rivalled that of Jameson and Guinness.

One of the highlights of a visit to Roe & Co is the blending lab experience, where you get to play the role of master blender. Blending is at once an art and a science and, for a brief moment, you are allowed a glimpse into this alchemy, learning about the importance of balance and how different flavour profiles – from the sweet and fruity to the rich and spicy – combine to create a perfect blend.

This hands-on experience is an exciting opportunity to experiment with different combinations and learn the nuances of blending, which is a crucial part of Irish whiskey production.

The tour also takes you through the working distillery, offering a close look at the copper pot stills and the distillation process. You'll learn about the triple-distillation method that is characteristic of Irish whiskey and how it contributes to the smoothness and complexity of the final product. There are three copper pot stills at Roe & Co; the middle, or intermediate still, is designed to give an extra layer of purification and sports a double boil ball to encourage reflex.

To top off the experience, the distillery has an elegant bar, The Power House, where you can sit back and enjoy a range of different cocktails made with the distillery's whiskey. The bartenders here are mixologists in every sense of the word, offering unique twists on classics while highlighting the whiskey's versatility. Whether you choose an old fashioned or something more experimental, the cocktails are a perfect way to conclude the tour.

Origins

The history of Roe & Co is deeply intertwined with Dublin's rich distilling heritage (see page 80). It dates back to the early 19th century when George Roe, a visionary distiller, transformed his family's small operation into one of the largest and most successful distilleries in Ireland.

Established in 1757 by Peter Roe, the family business grew under Peter's son George's leadership to dominate the Irish whiskey landscape, becoming one of the main producers, brokers and bottlers of whiskey in the world. By the mid-1800s, Roe's distillery, located in Dublin's Liberties district, covered 17 acres and produced an astonishing 9 million litres (2 million gallons) of whiskey annually. This made it the largest in Europe at the time.

Roe's distillery was famed for the towering windmill on its site, the remains of which can still be seen today. Built on the site in 1856, the windmill became an iconic symbol of the distillery's success and was visible across the city. Alongside Guinness and Powers, Roe was a powerhouse, with its whiskey exported worldwide.

However, tough times meant that by 1926 the once-mighty Roe & Co was forced to close its doors, and its name faded into history. That was until 2017, when the Roe & Co brand was revived by Johnnie Walker owners Diageo. The new distillery was built just steps away from the original one on the old Guinness Power Station, and reopened in 2019. Like Teeling, it is located in the historic and storied Liberties district which was once alive with the clang of barrels and the scent of malt, and has seen the rise and fall of many a distiller's dream. Today, it's a sleek, stylish whiskey distillery, and is a testament to Dublin's evolving relationship with both tradition and innovation in whiskey-making. Visiting the distillery offers a unique blend of history, craftsmanship and modern innovation, making it a must-see for both whiskey aficionados and casual tourists alike.

Roe & Co Irish Blended Whisky

45% ABV

The nose opens with floral notes of rose petals, copper and sweet fruits, enhanced by a hint of ginger that adds subtle spice and depth. These elements carry through to the palate, where you'll find flavours of fresh-cut flowers, passion fruit and kumquat. The finish is delightful, featuring gooseberry fool and gorse, rounding out the experience with a refreshing touch.

Roe & Co Solera Irish Single Malt Whisky

46% ABV

Delicate aromas of lily of the valley and daisy are complemented by soft hints of white musk and rich notes of orange-flavoured chocolate on the nose. A touch of vanilla leads the way on the palate, followed by creamy orange notes and a subtle layer of oak spice. The finish amplifies the fruity profile, introducing vibrant hints of guava and passion fruit for a bright, tropical conclusion.

17

Jameson Distillery Bow Street

BOW ST · SMITHFIELD · DUBLIN 7 · D07 N9VH · REPUBLIC OF IRELAND

The Jameson Distillery Bow Street has kept the home fires burning in Dublin, and has been a lighthouse for Irish whiskey in the city even when there were no distilleries making the liquid gold. Today, with the growth of the Jameson brand, this flagship location is home to a brilliant visitor's centre and maturation warehouse.

As you approach the distillery, its old brick façade gives you a sense of entering a place steeped in tradition. Inside, there is an atmosphere of pure conviviality at the bar, which greets you with the sound of cocktails being shaken. With dark wooden beams, exposed stone walls and the smell of whiskey gently lingering in the air, it feels like a perfect balance between the industrial

past and the modern visitor experience.

The tour experience here has been greatly invested in, and it is one of the best introductions to whiskey anywhere in the world. While the Jameson Distillery Bow Street no longer produces whiskey onsite, examples of copper pot stills, tools and equipment are here to be seen. The attention to detail in the explanations, combined with visual aids, multimedia and interactive elements makes the complex process of Irish whiskey production engaging and easy to understand.

There is also a maturation warehouse, which provides whiskey matured in the city for the Jameson 18 Years Old Bow Street Edition. Cocktails can be enjoyed at the bar and there is the opportunity to personalize a bottle of Jameson, making a unique souvenir. Distillery-only bottles are also available.

Origins

Scottish-born John Jameson founded his distillery on Bow Street in Dublin, in 1780. At the time, Dublin was a major centre of whiskey production. Throughout the 19th century, Jameson became one of Ireland's most successful whiskey producers, gaining a reputation worldwide and a famous label and bar-call.

In 1975, production of whiskey for the Jameson blend moved to the New Midleton distillery in County Cork, where the label continues to be made today. Despite these changes, Jameson remains one of the most iconic and best-selling Irish whiskeys, known for its consistent quality and smooth taste. It sells over 60 million bottles worldwide every year.

Distilling in Dublin, along with Irish whiskey itself, has undergone a revival over the last two decades, and the Jameson Distillery Bow Street has been a stalwart in the city. Located in the heart of Dublin's Smithfield district, it provides a captivating experience that offers a deep dive into the history and craftsmanship behind one of Ireland's most iconic whiskey brands. It also offers a look at the range of single pot still Irish whiskeys made at the Midleton distillery in County Cork (see page 82).

Jameson Bow Street 18

40% ABV

The nose opens with creamy coconut flesh and soft summer fruits, intermingled with dates. On the palate, ripe tropical fruits come forward, balanced by a touch of cracked black pepper and a subtle hint of tobacco. The finish brings a touch more fruit, with a delicate hint of spice that lingers on the palate.

Jameson Original

40% ABV

This has inviting aromas of light floral notes, apple juice, sweet citrus and a hint of vanilla. The palate features soft orchard fruits, vanilla and toasted brown bread, with a subtle spice. The finish gives a sweetness of cream soda and gentle warmth. Its approachable character and versatile nature has been the driver for the rebirth of Irish whiskey this century.

18

Tullamore D.E.W.

CLONMINCH · TULLAMORE · CO. OFFALY · R35 E027 · REPUBLIC OF IRELAND

The revival of Tullamore D.E.W. distillery needed to be done by a company that understands whiskey and the long-term investment in it. Step up William Grant & Sons, the owner of Glenfiddich and The Balvenie. Its vision is manifest in these two Scotch brands and provides an exciting platform for the rebirth of this much loved label.

Around 90 minutes drive from Dublin, upon arrival, the impressive distillery complex instantly catches your eye. The modern, glass-fronted visitor's centre contrasts with the surroundings' rural charm, symbolizing the fusion of traditional and contemporary techniques that defines Tullamore D.E.W. The warm welcome from the staff sets the tone for the visit, with a sense of pride in both the heritage of the brand and the craftsmanship behind their whiskey.

The tour begins with a deep dive into the distillery's history, which dates back to 1829 when the original company was founded. The brand's name is derived from Daniel E. Williams (D.E.W.), a visionary who joined the distillery in the late-19th century and eventually became its owner. Williams is credited with transforming Tullamore into one of the Ireland's most recognized whiskey brands – today it is the second biggest selling Irish blend, behind Jameson – introducing the now-famous slogan 'Give every man his D.E.W.'

The tour gives access to all three essential stages of production – malting, distilling and maturation – after a warming welcome with an Irish coffee. The distillery itself has a unique still set-up with exceedingly long lyne arms (see page 17). One of the highlights of the tour is the warehouse, where 50,000 casks lie quietly ageing away.

As the tour concludes, visitors are invited to relax in the Old Bonded Warehouse and the Tully Snug, a stylish bar and lounge area where you can enjoy a drink, purchase exclusive bottles, or simply reflect on the rich experience of the day.

The surrounding area also offers incredible natural beauty to explore, and the distillery provides great advice for walks in the local Slieve Bloom Mountains, or boating on the nearby River Shannon.

Origins

Tullamore D.E.W. takes its name from the nearby town of the same name in County Offaly, where the brand was first realized. The original distillery was founded in 1829 by Michael Molloy, a local businessman who recognized the growing demand for Irish whiskey. Under Molloy's stewardship the distillery thrived, producing fine whiskey for the domestic market.

After Molloy's death, the distillery ended up in the hands of Bernard Daly (when it was renamed Daly's distillery) and was written about in 1886 by whisky historian Alfred Barnard in this book *Whisky Distilleries of the United Kingdom*. (At this point in history, the island of Ireland was included in the wider realm of the United Kingdom.)

However, it wasn't until the arrival of Daniel E. Williams that Tullamore DEW truly flourished. Williams, who started working at the distillery in the late 1800s, eventually became the distillery's manager and, later, its owner. He modernized the site with electric lighting and expanded production. His initials were added to the brand, giving us the label we have today.

Tullamore DEW is one of Ireland's most iconic whiskey brands and is the first to have blended all three styles of Irish whiskey (single malt, pot still and grain). However, the company was left homeless from 1954 when Daly's distillery closed. Keeping pace with whiskey drinking trends, though, the brand remained alive and William Grant & Sons purchased the label in 2010.

In 2013, the owners broke ground on a new distillery at Clonminch, on the outskirts of the town of Tullamore. This freshly built distillery (which includes a mix of renovated old distillery buildings, and new builds, too) offers an experience that immerses visitors in the traditions of Irish whiskey-making, while showcasing the innovation that has kept this brand relevant for over 190 years.

Tullamore D.E.W. 18 Years Old

41.3% ABV

The nose opens with a coconut note paired with crisp apple juice, followed by subtle blackcurrant and a touch of pear drops. The oak presents a fruity character rather than a spiced one. On the palate, it's smooth and oily, with hints of dry sherry, salted meats and leather. The finish brings flavours of plums and figs, complemented by a touch of vanilla.

Tullamore D.E.W.

40% ABV

The nose offers the freshness of freshly cut grass, accompanied by sweet notes of breakfast tea, hints of minerals, wet sand and a touch of peach melba. On the palate, tropical fruits blend with red stone fruits and a delicate sweetness. The finish brings red apple and a warming touch of spiced cinnamon for a satisfying close.

19

Bushmills

2 DISTILLERY RD · BUSHMILLS · CO ANTRIM · BT57 8XH · NORTHERN IRELAND

Located against the rugged beauty of Northern Ireland's Causeway Coast, Bushmills is set in the heart of the bucolic village of the same name, just a few miles from the awe-inspiring Giant's Causeway. On a clear day, from this very northern part of the island of Ireland, you can even see Scotland's Campbeltown coastline (see page 111) as well as the famous whisky island of Islay (see page 110).

The village of Bushmills feels timeless; a quiet, sleepy place where the pace of life seems dictated by the rhythm of the distillery itself. The approach is part of the charm: narrow, hedge-lined country roads wind through a landscape of soft, undulating hills and verdant fields, with the ever-present scent of sea salt carried inland from the nearby Atlantic. Upon arrival at the distillery the stout, stone-clad site emerges like a guardian of history, its black-and-white façade immediately recognizable and deeply evocative. The success of Bushmills is evident in a new addition to the site: its ultra-modern, glass-clad Causeway distillery, which cost £37 million to build and opened in 2023, doubling the site's capacity for single malt production.

Inside the historical building, visitors are immersed in the whiskey-making process, guided through the stone-walled room, where the air is heavy with the earthy sweetness of barley. The barley, which is locally sourced, is mashed and fermented in the usual single malt style. The real point of difference comes in the old still house, where Bushmills employs a triple distillation method, leading to a spirit that's as light as silk. Bushmills takes its water from St Columb's Rill, a tributary of the Bush River, which contributes to all aspects of the process, from cooling to cutting.

Maturation is key for a triple-distilled spirit. Such a light spirit soaks in the essence of its surroundings, marked by the Atlantic breeze and the soft, temperate Irish climate, both of which contribute to a whiskey that is velvety and easy to drink.

Bushmills is bottled in two styles: as a blend and a single malt. The blended version (currently Red Bush, Original and Black Bush, along with some other limited releases) brings together the distillery's own malt with a portion of grain whiskey distilled elsewhere in Ireland. A true taste of the distillery, however, is to be found in their single malt release. Over the past decade the range and repertoire from Bushmills

has grown, and expressions can be found at various ages from ten years old through to over thirty years of age.

Origins

The history of Bushmills whiskey is deeply intertwined with the story of Ireland itself. Officially licensed in 1608, Bushmills holds the distinction of being the oldest licensed whiskey distillery in the world and has operated continuously for over four centuries, which is quite remarkable.

In 1608, King James I granted Sir Thomas Phillips, a local landowner, a licence to distil, marking the formal beginnings of what would become the Bushmills distillery. Through centuries of war, famine and political upheaval, Bushmills continued to produce its renowned whiskey, with the

local area becoming synonymous with quality spirit-making.

The distillery's first recorded major milestone came in 1784, when it officially registered as the Old Bushmills Distillery Company. In 1885, however, a fire destroyed much of the distillery, but it was rebuilt and production resumed.

The 19th century saw Bushmills grow in reputation, exporting its whiskey globally, especially to the United States where it was moved by paddle steamer from the northern coast of the island. This robust reputation saw the distillery survive the challenges of Prohibition (see page 22) in the United States, when sales of whiskey were severely restricted.

Despite the global demand for Bushmills whiskey remaining strong, and the overall growth of Irish whiskey since the turn of the century, Bushmills has found itself as the make-weight in several commercial deals. Formerly under the ownership of Irish Distillers (see page 80), it was sold to Scotch giant and Johnnie Walker owner Diageo in 2005. It was subsequently sold to Proximo Spirits, the family-owned business behind Jose Cuervo tequila. Today, Bushmills has remained steadfast, its triple-distilled whiskey known for its smoothness and quality.

Bushmills 12-Year-Old Single Malt

40% ABV

The nose reveals peach iced tea, cream soda, praline and hints of cocoa. There is some cinnamon and a dash of new leather, too. The palate has the signature Bushmills tropical fruit notes, along with runny honey and red apples. There is slight dry spice note, as well as toasted marshmallow. The finish lingers with warm notes of nutmeg and subtle salted caramel.

Bushmills 16-Year-Old Single Malt

40% ABV

A gentle giant, this expression opens with notes of sunflowers and ginger, evoking a summer's day in the garden with ginger tea and cinnamon buns. On the palate, it reveals rich strawberry jam, layered with hints of sherry and bourbon, underpinned by the subtle depth of high-quality loose leaf breakfast tea, without milk. The finish is delicate, offering soft cinnamon spice and a touch of crisp apple juice.

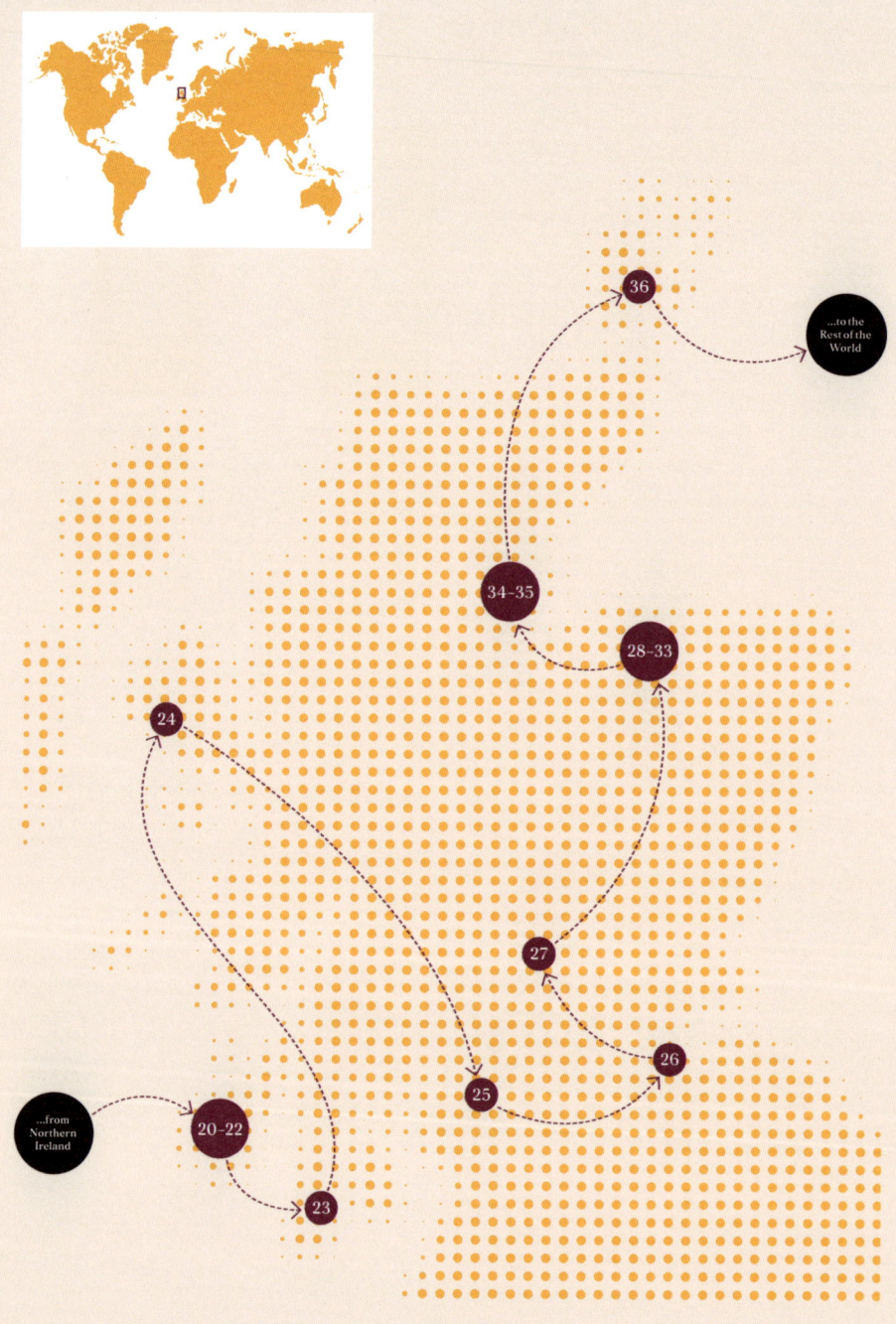

...from Northern Ireland

20-22

23

24

25

26

27

28-33

34-35

36

...to the Rest of the World

Scotland

A dispatch from Scotland

A brief history of Scottish whisky

Scotland is often considered the birthplace of whisky, but this is not entirely true. What Scotland can claim, however, is that whisky was first referenced in some of the country's official court documents. It was noted in the Exchequer Rolls in 1494 that Friar John Cor was to acquire 'eight bolls of malt wherewith to make aqua vitae' – aka whisky spirit.

In the half millennium since Friar Cor began distilling, the drink has undergone quite a revolution with Scotch becoming not just a household item, but a luxury one at that. The status of Scotch was first confirmed in 1822 when King George IV arrived in Scotland and called for a dram of 'Glenlivet whisky'. Was he asking specifically for The Glenlivet single malt itself? Sadly not. 'Glenlivet' was a term used for the malt whisky made in and around the area of the same name. Today, this location is known as Speyside and is home to such distilleries as The Macallan (see page 156) and The Balvenie (see page 152).

The main-stay of the Scotch category is blended Scotch whisky, which brings together liquid from Scotland's 140 plus single malt distillers, as well as grain whisky made on column stills, from other types of grains aside from malted barley. Famous names such as Ballantine's, Chivas Regal and Johnnie Walker (more about him on page 136) lead the way and have given life to myriad single malt distilleries across Scotland. As you visit these incredible producers, you'll hear stories of the blends they contribute to. Without these blends, many of the single malts would not exist.

This is not to say that Scotch has had an easy ride of it. Far from it. Many different factors have had serious effects on Scotch whisky. By the start of the 1980s, Scotch's fortunes had waned, supplanted by clear spirits such as vodka, which was increasing in popularity in the bars and clubs of the world's big cities. In an industry that has to be proactive in forecasting the future, the result was purely reactive: the closure of a number of distilleries. In total, 20 distilleries closed their gates in the 1980s, including the now storied names of Port Ellen (see page 116) and Brora. Seven more befell the same fate in the early 1990s; over the same period, just two new distilleries opened.

And this was not the first time that Scotland had seen a serious contraction of whisky production – it had become something of a trend in the industry. In the 1920s, 40 distilleries closed, a consequence of huge over-supply and Prohibition being invoked in North America. Boom years came later, though, with 22 sites opening between 1957 and 1976.

In the same way, the closures of the 1980s and 1990s preceded a new dawn for Scotch; as the 20th century drew to a close, more mature and educated whisky drinkers discovered the delights of single malts – and, with this, came a natural curiosity to try spirit from 'lost' distilleries.

Suddenly, single malts became fashionable. Between 2002 and 2016, exports grew by 143 per cent from 47 million bottles to 114 million, and the hidden gems made at mothballed or demolished distilleries developed legendary status, as did highly sought-after single malts such as Macallan and Bowmore.

It is this demand for quality whisky that has seen Scotland's distilleries focus on their visitor experiences, with them now being the biggest attraction in the country.

When to visit Scotland

Visiting Scotland's whisky distilleries is an experience that goes beyond just the drink itself; it's an immersion into the heart and soul of Scottish culture. If you want to capture the essence of what makes Scotland's whisky regions so enchanting, plan your visit around two key events: the Fèis Ìle and the Spirit of Speyside whisky festivals. These events offer unparalleled access to distilleries, exclusive tastings and a chance to connect with the passionate people who keep Scotland's whisky traditions alive. Many distilleries also offer exclusive bottlings to take home as mementoes of the pilgrimage.

Beyond the festivals, there's a timeless appeal to visiting Scotland's distilleries. There is no bad time to take in a two

Michelin-starred meal at The Glenturret (see page 140), or walk through the mist on the remote Isle of Skye as you sip a smoky Talisker (see page 128). The landscapes, the history and the sense of place you get from standing where countless casks have aged, drawing flavours from the wood and the air, are profound.

Each season brings its own charm, but my favourite time to visit is when the vibrant hues of September and October come out, and the verdant green Highlands have turned to a burnt amber shade. But the very best time to visit Scotland's whisky distilleries is whenever you can make the journey. You will be welcomed with open arms, and a dram in hand.

Fèis Ìle – Islay's Festival

Let's start with Islay's Fèis Ìle whisky festival. Held at the end of May, this week-long celebration transforms the remote island of Islay into a bustling hub of whisky enthusiasts from around the globe. Islay, known predominantly (but not exclusively) for its peaty and smoky whiskies, is home to some of Scotland's most iconic distilleries like Bowmore (see page 120), Ardbeg (see page 112) and Port Ellen (see page 116).

Imagine arriving at this rugged island, greeted by the briny sea air and the smell of peat fires burning in the distance. Each day of the festival is dedicated to a different distillery, offering exclusive tastings, behind-the-scenes tours and masterclasses led by the people who craft these legendary whiskies. The sense of community is palpable as you share drams with fellow aficionados, swap stories and savour the island's unique atmosphere.

But Fèis Ìle isn't just about whisky; it's about Islay itself. Take a moment to explore the island's windswept landscapes, ancient standing stones, charming villages and Islay Ales brewery. Attend traditional ceilidhs (Scottish social gatherings) where local

musicians play foot-stomping tunes that linger in your soul long after the music stops. It's an experience that connects you deeply with the spirit of Islay and its people.

Interestingly, the Fèis Ìle is preceded by the Campbeltown Whisky Festival which is conveniently on the Kintyre Peninsula where the ferry for Islay departs. If Springbank (see page 124), Glen Scotia and the rare, rich, oily malts of this region are your bag, then make sure you build in a trip down the Mull of Kintyre for this wonderful but short celebration of Campbeltown's malts.

Spirit of Speyside Whisky Festival

Now, let's head to the Highlands for the Spirit of Speyside Whisky Festival, typically held in late April to early May. Speyside, part of the vast Highland region, is made up of rolling valleys, towering mountains and crystal-clear rivers, and is the heartland of Scotch single malt whisky production.

Home to over half of Scotland's distilleries, including Glenfiddich (see page 148), The Macallan (see page 156) and the site that defines the region, The Glenlivet (see page 164), this part of Scotland is renowned for its smooth, rich, and often fruity whiskies.

The Spirit of Speyside festival offers a chance to hop from one historic distillery to another. The festival's events range from intimate tastings in centuries-old cellars, to guided walks through the picturesque Speyside landscape, where you can learn about the natural elements that influence the region's whisky.

20

Ardbeg

PORT ELLEN · ISLE OF ISLAY · ARGYLL · PA42 7EA · SCOTLAND

Few distilleries have quite the sense of self that Ardbeg has. It is a brand that does not take itself too seriously, but produces one of the most flavoursome whiskies in Scotland.

To pick just a couple of distilleries to visit on the island of Islay is like being asked to choose a favourite child. They are all so distinct, so welcoming, they all produce amazing whisky and are all incredibly welcoming to visitors. So, why Ardbeg?

Ardbeg is a magical place with incredible personality, to the point where it embodies all that this book is about. It is not a distillery that has focused on multi-million pound immersive displays, or modernist, moving exhibitions. What it does is focus purely on the welcome, and making you feel at home.

The distillery itself lies at the end of one of the most storied roads in Scotch history. It's a road that starts in Port Ellen (see page 116) and passes the new Portintruan distillery, famous Laphroaig, and the much loved and lauded Lagavulin. It then winds into Ardbeg on the island's south eastern Kildalton coast. From the sea, you'll spot its whitewashed walls and black-lettered name, shouting out loudly, 'A-R-D-B-E-G'.

The traditional visitor's centre starts with a café and shop, where the smiles are as warming as the drams they serve. The hearty local fare is always excellent and the perfect reward for reaching the end of a long, whisky-soaked road.

Tours are regular and take in the production, along with a tasting. You may even find yourself guided by the distillery manager, and this small site has a history of managers who are so proud of their distillery, they're keen to show it off themselves.

The distillery has recently doubled in size – although it is still small compared to others (2.5 million litres/550,000 gallons per annum maximum capacity, which is just under 10 per cent of Glenfiddich, for example) and has just two sets of stills. Ardbeg employs purifiers to aid reflux and spirit character in this highly peated whisky.

A 10-year-old expression has long been the calling card for Ardbeg, but it is also a place of fun experimentation, too, with regular limited-editions released to show off some of its more interesting whiskies. Peat smoke is not a flavour that is to everyone's taste but a visit to Ardbeg will have you falling in love with the place, the people and hopefully the peat, too.

Origins

The distillery's history dates back to 1815 when it was officially founded by John MacDougall, though illicit distillation had been taking place on the site long before. Ardbeg quickly established itself as a significant player in the whisky industry, thanks to the abundant peat bogs on Islay, which provided the fuel to create its famously smoky flavour.

During the 19th century, Ardbeg thrived as the demand for peated whisky grew and its location on Islay helped solidify its reputation. The distillery expanded throughout the late 1800s, reaching peak production in the early-20th century, when it was home to over a hundred people, a school, a post office and a bowling green.

However, like many distilleries, Ardbeg faced difficulties during the economic hardships of the early 1900s and the distillery's operations fluctuated throughout the 20th century with multiple closures and ownership changes. In 1981, Ardbeg shut down entirely and, for much of the 1980s and early-1990s, it operated only intermittently, producing whisky primarily for blending.

In 1997, luxury goods business LVMH, owners of Moët & Chandon, Hennessy Cognac and Glenmorangie (see page 172), acquired Ardbeg and reopened the site. A local hotel, the Islay Hotel, was purchased by Ardbeg, and transformed in 2025 into Ardbeg House, a luxury 12-bedroom hotel, featuring a courtyard bar and destination restaurant.

The distillery's unique style of heavily peated whisky, and its strong sense of identity, have drawn in a new generation of fans. Ardbeg's history is one of resilience, with the distillery overcoming significant challenges to become one of the most iconic names in Islay whisky.

Ardbeg 10-Year-Old Single Malt

46% ABV

Peat smoke and potpourri rise from the glass, reminiscent of a bonfire filled with heather, spices and a hint of tonic alongside frankincense. On the palate, it opens with notes of toffee apples, a touch of copper, rolling tobacco, honey and royal jelly. The finish brings subtle mossy undertones and crisp green apples, leaving a fresh yet earthy impression.

Ardbeg Uigeadail Single Malt

54.2% ABV

The nose opens with a smoky bonfire aroma, reminiscent of Victorian furniture, potpourri, incense sticks and frankincense, with a touch of toffee. On the palate, coppery tones blend with charred ends, rolling tobacco, pork crackling and a hint of honey mustard. Mossy notes, green peppers and layers of rich sherry and agave syrup are revealed for a complex and lingering close.

21

Port Ellen

KILN SQUARE · PORT ELLEN · ISLE OF ISLAY · PA42 7AF · SCOTLAND

There are few distillery names in the world of single malt Scotch whisky that excite as much as Port Ellen's. The iconic Islay distillery, beloved by many, reopened in 2024 with a focus on both the art of whisky-making and the science of smoke, boasting a design-led visitor's centre that reinvents the concept of the humble distillery tour.

The latter half of the 20th century was a challenging time for Scotch and the drink's fortunes waned in the late-1970s. As a result, 20 whisky distilleries had closed their gates in Scotland by the early 1980s, with seven more distilleries shutting shop in the early 1990s. In contrast, there were just two new openings in this time.

One of the casualties was the Isle of Islay's Port Ellen. However, when official bottlings of Port Ellen first appeared as a single malt in 2001 (as a 22 year-old with a price tag of around £100), drinkers were wowed and fans were made. Yet the distillery had been closed for 18 years. As more stocks from this 'ghosted distillery' started to appear, Port Ellen became something of a unicorn with smoky whisky drinkers and lovers of Islay malts.

In October 2017, Port Ellen's owner Diageo revealed plans to reopen the iconic distillery – although the process of resurrection has been a lengthy one. Seven years later in March 2024, and following a complete rebuild, spirit ran from the stills once again.

The rebirth of the Port Ellen saw two pairs of copper pot stills installed. One pair is an exact replica of the original copper pots, named the 'Phoenix Stills'. The other set is a smaller, experimental pair, designed to be adjusted and amended according to the distillers' needs.

The experimental stills at Port Ellen are fitted with a unique ten-part spirit safe that looks like a telephone exchange. This allows the distiller to section off the heart of the spirit run into smaller, more precise cuts. The aim is to develop an 'Atlas of Smoke', a map of different styles of smoky whisky.

Port Ellen is also home to a modernist visitor's centre with Scandinavian clean lines and Japanese design ascetics, all wrapped up in the warming, comforting tactile touches of Scotland. This is no haven for tartan and tweed but a well-thought through design statement. Tours start at £200 for a 90-minute immersive

experience with longer, bespoke visits available too.

Visitors to Islay often arrive through the town of Port Ellen, home to one of the island's two ferry ports, and pass the white-washed walls of the neighbouring Kildalton distilleries of Laphroaig, Lagavulin and Ardbeg (see page 112). All display their names in giant black stencilled letters. Today, the warehouse which proclaims 'Port Ellen' re-joins this canon of greats.

Origins

Port Ellen was originally opened in 1825 by Alexander Mackay on the site of a mill which, like the malting operation that exists there today, would have supplied malted barley to many of the whisky distillers on the island.

The business was not an instant success and, in 1836, the distillery reins were taken over by a 21-year-old gentleman called John Ramsay, the man who was to have a major impact on this port-side producer. Ramsay's vision was to establish Port Ellen as a serious whisky-making operation, to rival neighbouring Laphroaig, Lagavulin and Ardbeg.

Port Ellen was released unusually as a single malt and was one of the first to be exported to the USA under Ramsay's watch. His focus was not just on whisky-making, but embellishing the island's infrastructure, helping to start a bi-weekly steamership to and from Glasgow.

The Ramsay family controlled the distillery until 1920 when Port Ellen was purchased by the blending powerhouse duo of John Dewar and James Buchanan, and the very early beginning of the Distillers Company Limited, and later part of Diageo.

However, much like in the 1970s and 1980s, turbulent economic headwinds and Prohibition in America got the better of Port Ellen and it closed in 1930, remaining so until 1967. In 1973, the site was earmarked to become a sizeable maltings, which has been operational ever since. In 1983, Port Ellen closed once again. This time the stills were removed and the distillery's status changed from 'monthballed' to 'lost', until its ultimate reopening under new owners Diageo in 2024.

Port Ellen 44-Year-Old 1978 Gemini Original Cask

54.9% ABV

Classic Port Ellen notes of grapefruit pith, chamois leather, lemon drops and delicate mossy smoke. A hint of coastal salt with some hints of liquorice, with damp autumnal forest floor notes. A palate of new leather at first, which develops into rich, smoked crème anglaise and sweet barley water. The smoky notes are again delicate and earthy, with a slightly energizing note of eucalyptus. Lemon posset and finally a hint of coal dust moves into tropical fruits

Port Ellen 44-Year-Old 1978 Gemini Remnant Cask

53.6% ABV

Deep oak notes with old leather and cloves. Some star anise, black tea and oak-chipping smoke. Sweet sherry, cocoa nibs, a hint of meaty notes and some toffee on the nose. The palate gives earthy smoke at first, which gives way to lightly brewed coffee, black cherry, dark chocolate and candied walnuts. There are also some meaty notes that aren't typical in Port Ellen, which add body and texture. Fruity notes of summer berry compote and fresh strawberry before more of the earthy smoke comes through.

22

Bowmore

SCHOOL ST · BOWMORE · ISLE OF ISLAY · PA43 7JS · SCOTLAND

If a sense of place is key to a distillery's character and personality, then Bowmore is a wise old sea dog of a whisky. One of the oldest in Scotland, this Islay distillery produces a beautiful, floral, smoky spirit that is the delicate ying to the wild and rugged location's yang.

Bowmore is the capital of what is considered Scotland's whisky island, the isle of Islay. The famous Bowmore distillery has sat stoically on the town's shoreline since 1779, watching the waves crash onto the walls of the distillery's No.1 warehouse, Scotland's oldest and most indomitable whisky storehouse. The No.1 warehouse is home to Bowmore's rarest stocks of whisky, which are not just historical mementos of a time gone-by, but are examples of some of Scotland's oldest single malts, from one of its longest serving distilleries. And at high tide it sits below the sea level, giving a unique atmosphere.

This liquid library acts as a guide for future distilling, as Bowmore is one of only a handful of single malt distilleries to actively employ ancient techniques, such as floor-malting barley (see page 17), a painstaking, time consuming and expensive craft, mostly lost now to industrialization. Floor malting is one element that keeps alive the older style flavours, richness and texture that the team at Bowmore strive for in their single malt.

Bowmore is also famed for producing a lighter, soft, floral peat-smoked whisky. It's a real antidote to other smoky sorts, the kind that carries a more medicinal note, with sea spray and tar. The lightness of the floral-style smoke within Bowmore's whiskies is underpinned with a rich texture, created by slow distillation and long ageing in the highest quality oak casks. These techniques are a postcard from the past, a style that's nearly been forgotten to efficiency and industry, which has been kept alive in this most remote of places in a unique single malt.

Islay's most historical distillery, boasting the island's oldest stocks of single malt, Bowmore is a joy to visit. The distillery offers tours that showcase its age-old practices, as well as a bar and tasting room with views that stretch over Loch Indaal (a sea loch) to the opposite shore of the island. It's probably the best view of any tasting room in Scotland.

Bowmore's production has historically been inconsistent but under the new

ownership of Japan's Suntory, there is a focus on developing a spirit with old school characteristics of the delicate and floral peated malt, longer fermentation times and slow distillation on two sets of stills. Long maturation in sherry casks has also become a focus for the distillery.

Origins

One of Scotland's oldest distilleries, and certainly the oldest operational distillery on Islay, Bowmore dates back to 1779. Established by local merchant David Simpson, it was in the 19th century when the distillery experienced significant growth and development.

Ownership changed hands several times over the 1800s, with the distillery remaining a key player in the production of Scotch

whisky on Islay. By the early-20th century, Bowmore was well-established as one of the island's premier distilleries, known for its distinct balance of peat smoke and subtle fruity notes.

One of Bowmore's most notable historical contributions is its World War II legacy: during the war, the distillery was used by the British Royal Air Force as a base for seaplanes. Production of whisky was halted, but the distillery's infrastructure remained intact, allowing it to resume operations after the war ended. In 1963, the distillery was purchased by a company which became known as Morrison Bowmore Distillers and in 1994, Suntory, the Japanese beverage giant, took control. Today, Bowmore is renowned for having some of the oldest stocks of whisky in Scotland.

Bowmore 12-Year-Old Single Malt

40% ABV

The nose presents aromas of floral smoke, cherry juice and stone fruits, with a subtle touch of vintage leather. On the palate, the floral smoke returns, complemented by creamy white chocolate and freeze-dried raspberries. The finish is delicately spiced, with notes of cinnamon and a lingering hint of smoke.

Bowmore 15-Year-Old Single Malt

43% ABV

The nose opens with cherry, forest fruits and smoked heather, accompanied by a touch of dry moss. On the palate, you'll find flavours of blood oranges, milk chocolate, malted milk and a subtle hint of basil with fruit compote. The finish brings a unique blend of rich summer fruits, smoke and lingering forest fruits.

23

Springbank

WELL CLOSE · CAMPBELTOWN · PA28 6ET · SCOTLAND

There are many reasons to make the trip to Campbeltown, but first on the list is Springbank. Almost a working whisky museum, Springbank is lauded for its vintage-style single malt and authentic, historic working practices.

Campbeltown is not an easy place to get to by road. There are flights to the region from Glasgow; two a day, on small 19-seater planes called an Otter. As quick as this route is (under half an hour), I prefer the drive, which is two and a half hours longer. If all the roads are open, that is. Flying might be quicker but a car allows you to stock up on whisky – and you'll want to bring plenty back from Springbank and the other Campbeltown distilleries you visit.

Campbeltown has a long and illustrious history of whisky distilling (see overleaf). It was once a hotbed for unlicensed distillers to ply their trade, thanks to its perfect placement – far away from any major cities, but within easy reach of Glasgow and the Isle of Man (where plenty of illicit cargo was hidden) by boat.

Springbank itself, though, is the poster child for the region. Firstly, it has been incredibly robust, operating continuously since 1828 (and most likely way before that). When you visit (and you really must), you'll find all the classic cues: heavy stone walls, a courtyard and vintage equipment.

Yet stepping into Springbank feels like stepping back in time. There is no modern equipment. Not a computer screen in sight. Chalkboards, yes. Screens, not one.

All elements of the process are here. Local barley is used and malted onsite. Of course there is the mashing, fermentation, distillation and maturation, too. But they also bottle here, making this a genuine 'farmhouse' distillery. The set up is small, with under 500,000 litres (110,000 gallons) of spirit made a year. Add to this long maturation, an inefficient, historic process, and the losses from the 'angels' share', and you are not left with very much at the end of it.

In the distillery's three small stills, three different and distinct spirit styles are produced: Springbank, Longrow and Hazelburn. Each has its own unique character, with Springbank carrying oily, rich, malty and lightly peated notes; Longrow being peated; and Hazelburn, unpeated and triple distilled. The rich, unctuous and scarce nature of the single malts have earned it a dedicated following

among whisky connoisseurs. As a result, Springbank remains a symbol of craftsmanship and authenticity, continuing to produce some of the most revered single malts in the world.

The visitor experience is quaint and cute, and as personal and personable as the distillery itself. You'll learn things from this trip that other distilleries either won't show you, or can't show you because the techniques have been lost to efficiency over tradition. The distillery shop, where cask samples are readily sold in full-sized bottles, like a whisky lucky dip from a cage (known in whisky-geek circles as 'cage bottles' for this very reason), elicits queues around the courtyard and, during the Campbeltown Whisky Festival (see page 111), around the corner and down the street.

The distillery employs over a hundred people, which is probably around ten times more people per-gallon than in any other distillery in Scotland, if not the world. Visit. Buy. And spend money to keep the place alive. And, apart from your philanthropy, leave no trace. Walk away from it untouched, with a rare whisky heirloom you can hand down to another generation to admire, support and enjoy.

Origins

Springbank was founded by Archibald Mitchell and the distillery remained in the hands of his descendants, the Mitchell family, for nearly two centuries. Sadly, the last family member-owner, Hedley Wright, passed away aged 93 in 2023 leaving the distillery in trust. Its long history is closely tied to Campbeltown, which was once known as the 'whisky capital of the world'

Springbank
10 Years Old

46% ABV

The nose reveals warm notes of incense sticks and honey, complemented by tinned pineapple, freshly chopped red apples and a hint of cinnamon sticks. On the palate, sweetness shines through with touches of suede, leather and copper, transitioning into a rich finish of cherry jam.

Longrow Peated
Single Malt

46% ABV

The nose is dominated by chamois leather and smoke, with hints of old leather boots, dubbin and mossy undertones. The palate carries these earthy themes further, adding fresh soil, a touch of copper and the scent of dusty books. The finish is bold and lingering, featuring clove spices alongside a final hint of leather.

due to the vast number of distilleries that operated in the area during the 19th century and in the early-1800s when it was home to over 30 licences distilleries, and many more illegal ones.

Initial single malt Scotch from the early- to mid-1800s was a thick, rich, smoky, oily affair, built for mixing with honey, lemon, hot water and often spices. This style is typical of Campbeltown and, even today, the three current operational distilleries – Glen Scotia (also very much worth a visit), Glengyle (see below) and Springbank – produce possibly Scotland's most identifiable mainland malt.

The whisky industry in Campbeltown suffered a dramatic decline between the late-19th and mid-20th centuries, yet Springbank was one of only a handful of distilleries that survived. In 2000, the Mitchell family bought a closed distillery next door to Glengyle and restored and reopened it. It produces whisky for just three months a year. How very 'modern' Campbeltown.

24

Talisker

CARBOST · ISLE OF SKYE · IV47 8SR · SCOTLAND

Talisker's tagline is 'Made By The Sea', and this underscores both the smoky, maritime character of the spirit and the wild Atlantic location of the distillery on the Isle of Skye.

Nestled on the shores of Loch Harport, Talisker makes a distinct style of Scotch that is smoke-forward, yet distinctly coastal with a hint of salinity. It is loved around the world. So much so that Talisker sells in excess of four million bottles a year, and this remote island distillery attracts more than 65,000 visitors a year.

It is a whisky that captures a sense of place like no other. The barley used is a mix of 25 per cent unpeated malt, to 75 per cent peated malt. Five very tall copper pot stills are used in a large, warehouse-style still room, which contain a purifier element that creates greater reflux (see page 16), adding additional layers of character to the distillation. Crucially, the spirit stills use worm tubs (see page 17) which are located outdoors, giving a weightier spirit, with seasonal variations.

Talisker is a malt whisky that morphs with maturation, too. Younger expressions (eight was a standard release age for many years) are lithe and lively, with smoky energy. And the older it gets, the more it relaxes. It moves from a quick cigarette into an aged cigar. It

becomes considered, broad shouldered, wise. Talisker is a distillery with some good older stocks, reaching into four decades of age on occasion.

With so many visitors, the distillery experience is one of the very best in Scotland and has been heavily invested in by owners, Diageo. Those who arrive are welcomed in to shelter from the weather in a wood-clad reception, before various rooms are visited with multimedia displays of the island, the history and the production. Tours take in the production areas and there's a tasting, too. The distillery is also home to a small café and restaurant, which sits just opposite the main site and occasionally hosts pop-ups with well-known chefs who cook locally sourced seafood and other specialities. The shop is well stocked and includes a bottle-your-own offering.

Origins

The history of Talisker dates back to 1830. It was founded by Hugh and Kenneth MacAskill, brothers who arrived to farm the local area in 1825. Focused on growing their agricultural business, they saw distilling as another good form of income from the land, and founded the distillery in 1830.

By 1848 the brothers declared bankruptcy and lost the distillery to the banks; the new owners found it hard to make a remote island distillery work. It wasn't until 1880 that two whisky entrepreneurs, Roderick Kemp and Alexander Allen, arrived with a vision to make the site more accessible for export, building a pier to enable an easier path of exit for the whisky to their customer base.

In 1892, Kemp sold his share to buy The Macallan (see page 156) and, after Allen's death in 1895, his stake was taken up by his business partner, Thomas Mackenzie. In 1916, the group which owned Johnnie Walker, Dewars, and other major blended whisky brands, acquired the distillery. This group eventually became Diageo, who still own the distillery today. It wasn't plain sailing from there either: in 1960 the distillery burned down and was shuttered until 1962, when it was rebuilt.

Records show that Talisker whisky was once triple distilled but today is double distilled. The stalwart expression of Talisker is a 10-Year-Old, prized for its peaty, peppery and slightly salty and sweet notes, all underpinned by a distinctive maritime character. The Scottish islands have always been a hot-bed for distilling, providing typically hard to reach places that were, in turn, out of reach for many of the government agents employed to seek out illicit distilling. As such, the Isle of Skye provided an ideal place for a whisky distiller pre-legalization.

Talisker 10 Years Old

45.8% ABV

The nose opens with fresh mint and smouldering moss, accompanied by a subtle hint of bandages and pineapple – a curious but well-balanced combination. On the palate, smoked tropical fruits mingle with vanilla and delicate touches of oak. The finish is both sweet and smoky, reminiscent of a scoop of vanilla ice cream on a crisp Bonfire Night.

Talisker 18 Years Old

45.8% ABV

The nose features smoked mango, passion fruit and a hint of Jamaican pot still rum, leading into a palate of sweet mango, vanilla oak, rich red berries and creamy strawberry ice cream. The finish reveals mild spices alongside deep oak and smoke, creating a harmonious conclusion.

25

Auchentoshan

GREAT WESTERN RD · CLYDEBANK · G81 4SJ · SCOTLAND

Few distilleries in Scotland are as accessible as Auchentoshan, located on the outskirts of Glasgow. It is unusual in the canon of Scottish single malts, due to its history for triple distillation.

The unusually named Auchentoshan (Auch-en-tosh-an) is set among the rolling hills on the outskirts of Glasgow. The buildings are unassuming, almost humble, and their whitewashed walls and simple black slate roofs suggest an historic site that has let the city grow up around it.

Auchentoshan is a rare thing: a Lowland distillery. Once the hub of spirit production, the Lowlands now have the second fewest distilleries of any region after Campbeltown, and this is one of the flagships of the area. Auchentoshan, unlike its fellow Scotch single malt producers, is known for its triple distillation – a rare method in Scotland that gives its spirit a purity and refinement that stands apart from the heavier, peat-laden malts from the islands, or the rich, oily, heathy malts of the Highlands.

The set up is simple: three stills, with the spirit moving from the first (the wash still), to the intermediate, and then to the final distillation in the spirit still. With a cut point at a higher strength than double distilled whisky at 81 per cent ABV, it's almost 10 per cent higher than some other

malt distilleries. This triple distilled style used to be a signature of Lowland whiskies (with others such as Rosebank), but today there are only a handful of triple distilled whiskies in the country.

As a result, Auchentoshan's whisky works well long in cask, but it has to be handled with care. At such high distillation, the spirit is light and can be easily led by overactive barrels. It does, however, age well and this is seen across the range, which demonstrates a number of age statements as well as cask styles.

Due to the proximity to Glasgow, Auchentoshan attracts a large number of visitors each year. It is well set up for tours, with four versions currently available.

Origins

Auchentoshan distillery was founded in 1823. The distillery's name is derived from Gaelic, meaning 'corner of the field', reflecting the rural surroundings at the time of its conception. The same location could today be called 'urban'.

AUCHENTOSHAN
DISTILLED DIFFERENT
DISTILLERY AND VISITOR CENTRE

STILL HOUSE

During its early years, Auchentoshan changed ownership multiple times but remained a reliable producer of whisky, contributing to Scotland's reputation for high-quality spirits. Auchentoshan experienced significant hardship during World War II, when the distillery was badly damaged in 1941 by German bombing raids. The proximity to Clydebank, a hub of industrial activity and shipbuilding, made the area a target, and the distillery sustained extensive damage. Despite this, Auchentoshan was rebuilt and resumed production.

In 1969, the distillery was purchased by the Morrison family, and now finds itself under the ownership of Japanese drinks company, Suntory.

Auchentoshan 12 Years Old

40% ABV

Picture an orange grove with copper trees, gently kissed by rain – that's the essence of this whisky's nose. Adding apricots creates a captivating introduction to the palate, where rich, oily honey blends with Galia melon and subtle hints of cloves. The finish is enhanced by a warm touch of cinnamon.

Auchentoshan Three Wood

43% ABV

The Three Wood's nose is filled with rich aromas of caramel pudding, crème brûlée topping and sweet black tea. On the palate, there's a bold burst of spiced oak, cinnamon, nutmeg and cardamom. The finish offers a delicate hint of lavender and a touch of liquorice, adding an intriguing complexity.

26

Johnnie Walker Princes Street

145 PRINCES ST · EDINBURGH · EH2 4BL · SCOTLAND

Nothing highlights how big the world of 'whisky tourism' has become in Scotland, like the opening of the Johnnie Walker Experience on the busy thoroughfare of Princes Street in Edinburgh.

Let me get the obvious out of the way: this is not a distillery. However, it is one of the best places in the world to learn about Scotch whisky, from single malt through to blends, and should be on anyone's list of 'must visits' when touring Scotland's whisky producers.

As you stroll along Princes Street, with the majestic silhouette of Edinburgh Castle standing guard over the city, there is a stirring sense of history. Amid this venerable backdrop, the Johnnie Walker Experience sits like a modern cathedral to whisky, its sleek interior a striking contrast to the grandeur of its ancient surroundings.

Once a department store, this building is where the legacy of Scotland's most famous whisky unfolds, not in quiet reverence but in vibrant celebration of taste and discovery. The first thing you'll notice is the soft amber glow, which reflects the whisky itself, plus polished wood and glass – and a distinct lack of tartan. It speaks of both tradition and innovation. In the grand atrium, the history of Johnnie Walker comes alive.

As you ascend through the building on the guided tour, each floor offers a new chapter in whisky's tale. The immersive rooms bring you through the alchemy of blending – the art that made Johnnie Walker famous – while towering casks and glowing amber lights tell of the maturation process that takes place in the shadowy recesses of distilleries across Scotland. This site is also home to a bonded warehouse, allowing whisky to legally mature onsite.

Throughout the tour, whisky is served in various guises, mostly in Highballs (Scotch and soda), that aligns with the flavour profile you selected (from light and fruity, to rich and smoky, and in-between) when checking in. The building is crowned with the 1820 Rooftop tasting bar that has an unrivalled panoramic view of Edinburgh, where you can sip your whisky, have a cocktail or coffee, and watch the clouds roll in over Leith and into Edinburgh.

And so, with the glass in your hand and the city at your feet, you realise that the Johnnie Walker Experience is not only a celebration of whisky but a reflection of Scotland itself: proud, storied and alive with a deep and enduring spirit.

Origins

Johnnie Walker is perhaps the most iconic whisky brand in the world. It has a rich history that dates back to 1820, when a young John Walker opened a grocery store in the town of Kilmarnock, Scotland, after his father's death. While the store sold a wide range of goods, John Walker took a particular interest in tea and whisky blending. At that time, whisky was largely inconsistent in quality, with single malts often varying from bottle to bottle and the only way to ensure a consistent product for the customer was through blending, to achieve a more balanced, reliable flavour.

John's blending efforts became popular with his customers but it was after his death in 1857 that the Johnnie Walker brand truly began to take shape under his son, Alexander Walker, who inherited the family business. Alexander was a visionary and quickly saw the potential to expand the brand beyond Kilmarnock. He focused on marketing, branding and distribution, creating a product that appealed to a much wider audience.

One of Alexander's key innovations was the square bottle, introduced in 1860. This design was practical, as it allowed for more bottles to be packed into a crate, reducing breakage during transport. Around the same time, the distinctive slanted label was introduced, set at a 24-degree angle to stand out on the shelves. These two features became trademarks of the Johnnie Walker brand.

By 1867, Alexander launched the first commercial blend under the Johnnie Walker name, known as Old Highland Whisky. After Alexander's death, his sons,

Alexander II and George Walker, took over and further expanded the business. They were instrumental in turning Johnnie Walker into a global brand, using their father's innovations to build a reputation that extended far beyond Scotland.

In 1909, the company made a key decision to rebrand its whiskies using the colour-coded labels and the 'Striding Man' logo was created in 1908 by cartoonist Tom Browne. In the 20th century, Johnnie Walker became a leader in the whisky industry, expanding its range to include more labels like Green, Gold and Blue. Today, it remains one of the best-selling Scotch whiskies worldwide, known for its distinctive blends, innovative marketing and enduring legacy.

Johnnie Walker Blue Label Blended Scotch

40% ABV

The nose presents gentle vanilla peat smoke, complemented by notes of lanolin and lily, along with hints of strawberry and lime. On the palate, the vanilla peat is enriched with lavender and additional white flowers, finishing with subtle hints of spice and oak.

Johnnie Walker Black Label 12 Year Old Blended Scotch

40% ABV

Initial aromas of light smoke (mossy), dried fruit and hints of vanilla with just a wisp of honey and toffee. On the palate, this whisky delivers layers of dark chocolate, caramel and sweet spices, balanced by a distinctive smoky undertone. The finish is smooth and velvety, with flavours of oak, malt and subtle spices, which is long and warming.

27

The Glenturret

THE HOSH · CRIEFF · PERTHSHIRE · PH7 4HA · SCOTLAND

Flavour is key to any whisky distillery, but not many can boast a Michelin-starred restaurant alongside their maturing casks. The Glenturret can.

This historic distillery is one of the smaller producers in Scotland, with an annual output of around 400,000 litres (88,000 gallons), and there are multiple reasons why it should be on everyone's list of the most desirable distilleries to visit.

Its location, near Crieff in the Perthshire region of Scotland, is one of the country's most historic and picturesque areas, but it's also easy to access from Edinburgh and Glasgow. There's the added bonus of it being a hop-skip-and-jump from the fantastic Gleneagles Hotel, too, making it a true destination for anyone nipping to Scotland for a short trip.

To add to this, the distillery has undergone a transformation in the last few years. The distilling side remained somewhat stoic, leaning into the extreme history of this place; it has retained a small batch production which used to carry across both peated and unpeated styles. However, starting in 2025, the distillery is no longer using any peated malt at all, with an aim to focus entirely on making a light and fruity single malt that has been the main signature house style for over 260 years. In 2019, though, The Glenturret was purchased by luxury house, the Swiss based Lalique Group, who has focused on making the visitor's experience one of the most desirable in Scotland.

First, they brought in lauded whisky-maker Bob Delgarno, formerly of The Macallan and a man whose reputation is writ large in Scottish whisky. He has looked at stocks, albeit the highly limited nature of them, and reengineered the whiskies to bring the very best out of them, and give The Glenturret drinker a real treat. Secondly, the owners were keen to build a dining experience at the distillery with Scottish chef Mark Donald joining the new kitchen in 2021. The Glenturret Lalique Restaurant landed its first Michelin star in Donald's inaugural year, followed by a second. It is the only distillery-restaurant in the world with this accolade.

Other ventures include Aberturret Estate House, a luxury guest house that sleeps 12 guests that can be hired for overnight stays and longer visits, and The Glenturret's house gin. Named for the guesthouse, the gin uses the new-make spirit from the whisky distillery for extra body and texture, with botanicals foraged by Chef Donald.

Origins

The Glenturret is widely regarded as Scotland's oldest working whisky distillery, with its conception traced back to 1763, when a distillery on the same site, named Thurot, was operational. Eventually, it became known as The Hosh Distillery, named after the surrounding area and, by the early-19th century, the distillery had gained a reputation for producing high-quality whisky. It officially became known as The Glenturret in 1875.

The Glenturret closed its doors for several years in the 1920s, during the USA's Prohibition era and a general decline in whisky demand. It remained closed until 1957, when it was revived by whisky enthusiast James Fairlie, who restored the distillery and returned it to full production.

In 1981 French company Remy-Cointreau took control of the distillery and in 1990 the distillery was acquired by Highland Distillers, which later became part of the Edrington Group, owners of The Macallan (see page 156) and Highland Park (see page 176) when it became the spiritual home of The Famous Grouse.

In 2019, The Glenturret was purchased by the Lalique Group, marking a significant shift in the distillery's focus. With Lalique's influence, The Glenturret has embraced its luxury heritage, elevating its single malts to a new level of prestige. The distillery has since launched several premium expressions, showcasing its craftsmanship and commitment to quality.

The Glenturret 12 Years Old

46% ABV (2024 RELEASE)

A lovely note of plum jam, brambles, a hint of cocoa and some sweet praline notes. Some almond and a hint of cinnamon and leather. A drying yet sweet sherry note and some lovely ginger and dark chocolate tones, accompanied by a waft of cigar wrapper. A soft palate starts off with toasted walnuts and develops into the lightly charred top of a crème brûlée, with a hint of Madagascan vanilla and some deep, rich mahogany notes. A fruity, jammy flavour sits in the middle of the palate drawing all the flavours together.

The Glenturret 15 Years Old

50.8% ABV (2024 RELEASE)

The nose starts with aromas of candied orange and rosewater, with a hint of plum jam. Some strawberry notes are followed by cloves and vanilla with a touch of star anise. There are also deeper oaky notes as the whisky develops in glass, and a top note of licorice. The palate gives rich summer fruits of strawberry, blackcurrant and some blueberries, too, with a touch of fig and some honey sweetness. The finish is long and lingers with cloves again, and blackcurrant jam. A final note of hazelnut and dark chocolate finish this whisky off well.

28

Strathisla

SEAFIELD AVE · BANFFSHIRE · AB55 5BS · SCOTLAND

If there was a prize for the most picturesque distillery, not just in Scotland, but in the world, Strathisla would take the crown. It's a stunning distillery that makes first class whisky and is a must visit on any trip to the Scottish Highlands.

Strathisla distillery is located in the town of Keith, on the main road that runs from Aberdeen to Inverness, and through the Speyside region. Often hailed as one of the most picturesque distilleries in the country, despite being located in a town, Strathisla is surrounded by lush gardens, and the River Isla runs past the site.

It's immediately identifiable by its iconic twin pagoda chimneys, followed by a giant red waterwheel, which was historically used to power the site. It is listed as one of Scotland's oldest working distilleries, alongside The Glenturret (see page 140) and Bowmore (see page 120).

What makes Strathisla such a wonderful distillery to visit is the entire experience of the place itself. From the cobblestone courtyard through to the sumptuous and relaxing cottage-like interiors, it welcomes visitors in, and is a haven for those on the long journey through Speyside.

Tours here have two focuses: single malts and blends. Strathisla is the home of Chivas Regal, one of the world's best-selling blended Scotch whiskies, and Royal Salute,

an ultra-premium blend which starts life at 21 years of age. Here you can learn what goes into making a blended whisky, with a particular focus on Chivas Regal itself. This makes a tour of Strathisla unique, as it is keen not to just focus on its own whiskies, but also others from around Scotland. For example, its Warehouse No.3 tour covers malt whiskies from both Strathisla and sister distillery Longmorn.

The distillery is also home to a fantastic blending room, where guests can learn to create their own blended Scotch. In the interactive workshop, two examples of Chivas Regal with quite different flavour profiles are sampled, before exploring component parts, such as single malt and grain whiskies. Finally, you get to create your very own unique blend to take home in a 20cl bottle.

If you are feeling flush, the distillery offers The Vault tour, which is a half day immersion into the distillery with some of the rarest whiskies the company has to offer. It is bookable six weeks in advance.

The distillery is a wonderful place, and tours take in the small-scale production process. Home to just one pair of copper pot stills, smaller than most in the region, it produces a signature single malt that is smooth, rich and full-bodied, with notes of dried fruit, nuts and warm spices.

Although it is one of the core single malts in the Chivas Regal blends, Strathisla's own single malt expressions have earned a loyal following. The combination of its historic setting, traditional production methods and high-quality ingredients make Strathisla a standout distillery in the Speyside region.

Origins

Strathisla is the oldest continuously operating distillery in the Speyside region of Scotland, founded in 1786 by George

Taylor and Alexander Milne under the name Milltown Distillery. The location in Keith was chosen for its proximity to both the River Isla and the fertile barley fields of Speyside. At the time, whisky distilling was becoming increasingly popular, particularly in Speyside, which would later become the heart of Scotland's whisky industry.

In its early years, Strathisla (then Milltown) faced the same challenges as many other distilleries, including fluctuating demand and changes in regulation. However, it managed to establish a reputation for producing high-quality whisky, which helped it endure the tough years. In 1870, the distillery was renamed Strathisla, after the river that flows nearby.

In 1876 a fire destroyed much of the distillery, but it was quickly rebuilt and resumed production. The distillery continued to grow in the late-19th and early-20th centuries, adapting to changes in the whisky industry and maintaining its high standards of quality.

By the mid-20th century, Strathisla had fallen on hard times, and in 1940, it was forced into bankruptcy. Fortunately, in 1950, the distillery was purchased by Canadian entrepreneur Samuel Bronfman, the head of Seagram's, who was looking for a source of high-quality malt whisky to blend into the company's Chivas Regal line. They paid just £71,000 for the distillery. In 2001, French company Pernod Ricard acquired Seagram's, and with it the Chivas Brothers portfolio. Pernod Ricard continues to own and operate the distillery today.

Royal Salute 21
40% ABV

The nose gives aromas of Seville oranges, maple syrup drizzled over banana slices and vanilla ice cream topped with toasted hazelnuts, as well as tobacco and old leather chairs, and some sherry and spices. A sweet palate of apricots in syrup and crepe suzette is underpinned with pecan pie and salted caramel ice cream. There are hints of summer fruit fool and more maple syrup, too. A spiced finish has notes of dark cherry stones, toasted marshmallow and oak.

Chivas Regal 12 Years Old
40% ABV

Imagine sandy beaches in autumn, accompanied by a hint of sea spray, a hot lemon and sugar pancake in hand, and a pint of warm local ale. The palate mirrors this sweetness with an oily, mouth-coating texture that reveals flavours of apricots, lychee, summer berries and honey. The finish lingers with notes of sweet green tea.

29

Glenfiddich

Glenfiddich is one of the world's most renowned single malt whisky producers. Family-owned since 1886, it offers visitors a comprehensive and engaging distillery experience in the heart of Speyside.

The Glenfiddich distillery has established itself as one of the essential stops on any visit to the Speyside region and it was the first to open a visitor's centre in 1969. A famous name in the world of single malt Scotch whisky, Glenfiddich has also played a key role in the modern development of the category, and can be lauded for being the first regularly commercially available single malt Scotch globally.

On the approach to the Dufftown-based distillery, iconic pagoda roofs rise above the lush Scottish landscape and guide you in through a reassuringly large car park. It sets the tone, confirming that the public are very much welcome here. Glenfiddich has a modern visitor's centre, where the distillery's rich history is brought to life along with the story of William Grant, who founded the site in 1886 with the dream of creating 'the best dram in the valley'.

The distillery itself is, along with fellow Speysider The Glenlivet, one of the largest in Scotland: it has 43 copper pot stills (16 wash stills and 27 spirit stills), which combined gives Glenfiddich a production capacity of 21 million litres (4.6 million gallons) of alcohol a year.

The Glenfiddich whisky style is light and fruity, which leads to a Scotch that matures well and is easy to drink. It meets William Grant's vision, and has consistently been one of the biggest-selling single malt Scotch brands in the world.

Glenfiddich employs solera vats – large wooden vessels – and marrying tuns in the maturation process for their 15 Year Old and Perpetual Collection. These are used to store and marry liquid post-maturation, allowing the whisky to relax further before bottling, while always retaining a portion of liquid from previous vattings.

Unlike its next-door neighbour and sister distillery The Balvenie (see page 152), tours at Glenfiddich are regular and last anywhere between 90 minutes and four hours depending on your appetite for depth of knowledge. They run seven days a week, too.

The distillery also houses an excellent restaurant, offering locally sourced Scottish cuisine paired with Glenfiddich

whiskies and a well-stocked gift shop. The latter offers a wide range of Glenfiddich expressions, including some distillery exclusives. The opportunity to hand-fill and label your own bottle from a selected cask is a popular souvenir option. The distillery is well-equipped to handle large numbers of visitors, but booking in advance is still recommended, especially during peak tourist seasons.

Origins

Scotch whisky has a lot to thank William Grant for. Working at the Mortlach distillery, where he learned the ins and outs of distilling, he was keen to open his own site – Glenfiddich. After a year of hard work the first drop of spirit fell from the copper stills on Christmas Day 1887.

Before the advent of single malt as a category, malt distillers sold 100 per cent of their production to blending houses, and Glenfiddich was no exception. However, after a number of Grant's customers filed for bankruptcy in an aggressive marketplace in the late 1800s, he started the blend which carried his name: Grants.

Always keen to push whisky forward, it was Glenfiddich and the William Grant & Sons company, which is still family owned today, who developed and pioneered the commercial single malt whisky category. They sold Glenfiddich as a single malt from 1961, calling it 'Straight Malt' in what is now Glenfiddich's signature triangular bottle. This was a highly unusual move, with blends dominating the whisky scene. It was a move born of bravery, and it paid off: today Glenfiddich sells over one million cases (12 million bottles) a year. Such is the dedication and vision at Glenfiddich that it is one of the few distilleries to count a 40- and 50-year-old whisky as part of its core range.

Glenfiddich 15 Years Old

40% ABV

The aroma combines the essence of a jam-filled doughnut with the fresh scent of a flower show in the rain. This nose is rich with complex elements, featuring vibrant floral notes and hints of cinnamon spice. The palate mirrors this complexity, introducing a touch of jerk seasoning for added depth. The finish is slightly salty, accompanied by fruity notes, including freeze-dried raspberries.

Glenfiddich 18 Years Old

40% ABV

The nose is light and inviting, showcasing orchids and orchard fruits that evolve into notes of dried rose petals and trail mix. The oak is noticeable yet not overwhelming, allowing the palate to shine with a nutty essence reminiscent of Crunchy Nut Cornflakes, along with hints of ginger cake. The finish is dominated by ginger, featuring a fiery kick and subtle tones of green chilli.

30

The Balvenie

DUFFTOWN · BANFFSHIRE · AB55 4BB · SCOTLAND

One of Scotland's gems, The Balvenie distillery is a real treat for those who love traditional methods, as one of just a handful to employ their own floor maltings.

Located in Dufftown, the whisky capital of Scotland, The Balvenie sits as the neighbour to Glenfiddich (both under the same family ownership) on the road from Dufftown out to Craigellachie. The distillery offers whisky enthusiasts a unique and intimate look into traditional Scotch production. Unlike many modern distilleries, The Balvenie maintains its own floor maltings (see page 17), one of only a handful in Scotland to do so. This commitment to tradition is evident throughout the cosy visitor experience.

In contrast to its next-door neighbour, The Balvenie is a smaller distillery and a more boutique brand in the world of single malt. As such, tours – open to all – are deliberately restricted to just eight people, twice a day. This is not a place full of coach parties and animated videos of whisky-making. It is very much an exclusive experience for those keen to see behind the curtain of an historic Scotch distillery. As such, with a more personalized and intimate experience, booking in advance is essential.

The tour takes in all aspects of the whisky-making process, starting with the malting floors. Here, you can witness the labour-

intensive process firsthand, turning barley into malt – a practice largely abandoned by other distilleries – and touch, feel, taste and smell the home-malted barley. With a production capacity of around 4 million litres (880,000 gallons) per annum, the barley malted here accounts for around 15 per cent of the total needs of the distillery, but plays a vital role in the overall flavour and texture of the whisky. A portion of its own malted barley is used in every batch made.

The distillery itself is testament to the dedication of the Grant family and The Balvenie's owner's commitment to craftsmanship. The tour also takes in the distillery's onsite cooperage, which boasts a team of 20 and where you can see cask maintenance by hand.

The whisky made at The Balvenie is predominantly unpeated, and it is famed for its rich, smooth notes and finishing in sherry casks (double wood, as they call it). However, each year a small amount of smoky whisky is made, and this is bottled under The Balvenie brand, too.

The tour also takes in the site's legendary Warehouse 24, home to some of the

oldest and rarest casks that the distillery is maturing. An intimate whisky tasting concludes the tour, where five expressions are sampled.

Origins

The Balvenie was founded in 1892 when William Grant converted a farmhouse into a distillery, on a site next door to his newly opened Glenfiddich distillery (see page 148). The first distillation took place in May 1893, establishing the reputation of the single malt within the blending community as a first-grade spirit.

Between 1957 and 1971, the distillery underwent expansion, moving from just two stills to six (there are now five more, a total of 11, which is unusual as stills are usually found in even numbers, or working in pairs).

In 1973 the first official bottling of The Balvenie appeared, and then a regular offering 'Founder's Reserve' was launched in 1982.

The distillery's former Malt Master, David Stewart MBE (who retired 2023 after 60 years at the distillery), was one of the pioneers of double maturation, moving mature whisky from one style of cask, to another more active cask for a period of 'finishing'. This technique provided the foundation for the incredibly successful flagship bottling, The Balvenie 12-Year-Old Doublewood, which is first matured in a refill American oak cask, before a period in European Oloroso sherry butts.

The Balvenie is one of the few Scotch distilleries with very old stocks, and has a programme of releasing 50-year-old expressions on a semi-regular basis, as well as a number of vintages from across the middle of the 20th century.

The Balvenie 12-Year-Old Doublewood

40% ABV

The nose opens with runny honey and sweet vanilla, accompanied by a hint of oak, all perfectly balanced with a touch of spice. On the palate, deep oak mingles with vanilla, revealing notes of burnt sugar and coffee. The finish highlights spices and dark chocolate, adding a rich complexity.

The Balvenie 14-Year-Old Caribbean Cask

43% ABV

The nose evokes pure pineapple upside-down cake, reminiscent of rain transforming into honey over a pineapple field. This is further enriched by notes of mango and papaya. The palate mirrors the depth of the nose, introducing the flavours of ripe banana and blood orange. The finish is perfectly balanced, with a hint of spice and clove enhancing the tropical fruit notes.

31

The Macallan

EASTER ELCHIES · CRAIGELLACHIE · AB38 9RX · SCOTLAND

Nestled in the heart of Speyside, The Macallan offers visitors a truly extraordinary experience. The journey begins when you are welcomed by giant iron gates, standing sentinel at the entrance, which open to reveal a road that winds down into a 485-acre estate, woven into the breathtaking landscape of rolling hills and lush greenery.

Despite being located on the northern side of the River Spey in Speyside, the distillery leans on the more historic 'Highland' denomination for its labels.

As you approach the stunning modern distillery, with its undulating grass-covered roof that blends seamlessly with the surrounding landscape, you'll see that this architectural marvel, opened in 2018, is unlike any other in Scotland. A testament to The Macallan's commitment to innovation, this new facility sits in stark contrast to the site's age-old, whitewashed Georgian manor house. Built in 1700, the Easter Elchies House is the icon of The Macallan, and sits between the modern facility and mid-century distilleries, the latter of which is now decommissioned. The original distillery building stands as a testament to progress. Where other brands would have expanded an old site, the team at The Macallan have pushed ahead with a literally groundbreaking state-of-the-art subterranean operation.

The new site houses an all singing, all dancing visitor experience, offering guests an immersive journey into the world of whisky production and a captivating view of the Speyside landscape. One of the key pillars of The Macallan's flavour profile is its 'curiously small stills', which are on display. Currently, 32 stills produce the bold new make that The Macallan matures in sherry-seasoned casks.The tours also incorporate interactive elements, allowing visitors to see, smell and truly engage with the whisky-making journey. Sophisticated technology enhances the experience.

For those seeking a more luxurious experience, The Macallan offers the Mastery Tour. This premium option includes a gourmet lunch with paired wines, followed by an in-depth tour and tasting of some of The Macallan's finest and rarest whiskies in the atmospheric private tasting room, Cave Privée, where you are surrounded by maturing casks. The tour concludes with a personalized shopping

opportunity in the distillery's boutique. The Macallan is more than just a distillery; it is a modernist masterpiece, and a true whisky experience.

Origins

One of the original farm distilleries of the Highlands, The Macallan was legally registered in 1824 when Alexander Reid was granted a licence to make whisky. By 1892, the distillery was under the ownership of one of the Victorian distilling giants, Roderick Kemp, who previously owned Talisker (see page 128). The distillery stayed in the same family until the 1996 takeover by Edrington.

Between the 1960s and 1970s, significant investment was made with the number of copper pot stills, reaching 21 by 1975. This

growth was driven by increasing demand, particularly from the blended whisky market, where The Macallan became a sought-after component for blends like The Famous Grouse.

In the early 1980s, The Macallan moved to focus on the single malt market. The distillery released its first official single malt bottling in 1984, an 18-year-old expression matured in former sherry casks. It was this period that it gained its reputation as the 'Rolls Royce of Scotch', a term coined by whisky writer Michael Jackson.

This move would prove pivotal in establishing The Macallan's reputation as a premium single malt producer and, over the last 40 years, it has become the most collectable single malt Scotch in the world. It is one of the few Scottish single malt distilleries with very old aged stocks, and recent years have seen releases up to 83 years of age. This has helped to establish The Macallan as one of the most collectable and valuable single malts around.

The Macallan is currently under the charge of the Edrington Group, part of a family-owned charitable trust, alongside minority shareholders Scotland's William Grant & Sons (see pages 98 and 151) and Japan's Suntory (see page 226). The distillery's journey from humble farm distillery to global icon is an impressive one.

The Macallan Sherry Oak 12 Years Old

40% ABV

The nose begins with a harmonious blend of rich, ripe red fruits, deep oak and vanilla spices. On the palate, these flavours evolve into notes of damson, fig, and Parma ham. The finish is rich and rounded, featuring hints of pine oil, rancio and a touch of barbecue sauce.

The Macallan Sherry Oak 18 Years Old

43% ABV

The nose features red berries and dry sherry notes, complemented by hints of dry forest floor and autumn leaves. On the palate, it is unctuous and bursting with dark cherries, rich Madagascan vanilla and candied orange peel. The finish is enhanced by notes of cinnamon and mandarin.

32

Glen Grant

ROTHES · ABERLOUR · AB38 7BS · SCOTLAND

Most distilleries in Scotland are built around a central courtyard with whitewashed walls and possibly a view out to sea, or up a valley. None have manicured gardens and a lush, verdant estate like Glen Grant.

The Glen Grant distillery is quite a remarkable place. There are moments when, as you stroll around the exotic grounds, you could quite easily be standing in a Japanese distillery, as a waterfall tumbles in the background and wooden stairs lift you over deep, green, moss-covered rocks.

In the unassuming town of Rothes, just down the road from The Macallan (see page 156) and fed by the River Spey, Glen Grant is a pandora's box. When you arrive, it seems like there are many others in the area, with distillery buildings dotted around, still humming away making spirits. However, the first thing you notice on a tour is quite how clean and neat the place is, especially for an historic site.

This is the legacy firstly of the founders, James and John Grant, who were engineers to their core. Latterly, the site has been kept as new by Dennis Malcolm OBE, who was born at the distillery in 1946 and started working at Glen Grant in 1961. He retired in 2024 after 63 years as the guardian of the site.

The distillery, which makes a delicate, silky single malt, relies on four pairs of still. Unusually, all of them – both wash and spirit stills – are fitted with purifiers for additional spirit character and reflux, as well as vertical sides at the base of the neck of each still.

As impressive as the distillery and its whisky is, the gardens are the real superstar. The estate was developed to incorporate a huge greenhouse complex, along with extensive formal gardens. Founder James Grant's son, also called James but known as 'The Major', took charge of the business in 1872. He was an avid traveller and, when he returned from selling Glen Grant abroad, he often brought spectacular exotic plants and trees with him, many of which are still in the gardens today. The distillery calls the Victorian gardens 'a collection of natural grandeur unlike any other', and this is not just marketing bumph. It really is a magical place.

Tours are regular, and the visitor's centre has undergone a recent refurbishment. Glen Grant has a history of being drinkable at a

range of ages, and a five-year-old is a core expression in Italy. It also ages very well, with expressions aged for well over 30 years on the market.

Origins

Glen Grant was founded by brothers John and James Grant, who were versed in distilling and owned another whisky-making operation in the Elgin region. Glen Grant became known for its innovation and forward-thinking approach. In 1861, it was the first in Scotland to install electric lighting, while James 'The Major' Grant, son of founder James Grant, introduced tall, slender stills with purifiers. These created a lighter, crisp style of whisky, setting Glen Grant apart from many other Scotch distilleries known for producing heavier,

smokier malts. The Major was also the first man in the region to own a motor car.

Ever the innovator, in 1898, The Major built a second distillery across the road from Glen Grant, called Glen Grant No. 2; it sadly failed and closed after just four years. The distillery operated intermittently from 1965 (renamed Caperdonich) but was demolished in 2010 after it closed fully in 2001.

This reputation for innovation and modern technology led to Glen Grant's popularity and, under The Major's leadership, demand rose internationally, especially in Italy, where the whisky became immensely popular and is still the biggest selling single malt in the country. In 1978, the distillery was acquired by the Italian drinks company Gruppo Campari, further strengthening its connection with the Italian market. It remains part of the group today.

Glen Grant
10 Years Old

40% ABV

The nose opens with vanilla, which evolves into notes of nectarine and blood orange, accompanied by a touch of red fruits. On the palate, additional spice and oak notes complement the fruity aromas from the nose. The finish reveals a hint of sweetness, returning to the bright essence of blood orange.

Glen Grant
18 Years Old

43% ABV

An extraordinary bouquet of freshly cut flowers, reminiscent of an autumn meadow, mingles with ripe stone fruits and a hint of spice. The palate is rich and oily, showcasing more stone fruits along with elements of dry sherry. The finish is robust and lingering.

33

The Glenlivet

BALLINDALLOCH · BANFFSHIRE · AB37 9DB · SCOTLAND

The Glenlivet distillery was the forerunner for legal distillation in the Scottish Highlands, and today is one of the most established single malt Scotch brands.

Boasting a fantastic history and heritage, The Glenlivet distillery sits in the picturesque Livet Valley and has built an exceptional visitor offering to showcase its journey to one of the best-selling single malts.

Tours are regular and involved, with guests experiencing a blend of history and modernity. One of the most famous names in Scotch whisky, The Glenlivet has expanded its operation over the last decade or so, with brand new still houses sitting in contrast to the main distillery buildings from the 20th century. Now with a potential production capacity of 21 million litres (4.6 million gallons) per annum, it is the largest single malt distillery in the world, alongside fellow Speyside distillers Glenfiddich (see page 148).

The visitor experience begins at the modern and inviting visitor's centre. Here, interactive displays and historical artefacts tell the story of The Glenlivet's founding in the hills above the current distillery, alongside documents showing off the first licence to distil, which was issued to the then owner George Smith in 1824.

The distillery is equipped with an astonishing 14 pairs of stills, creating a whisky that is driven by tropical fruits and bananas. This easy drinking style has won fans the world over. The tours include immersive multi-sensory rooms to delve deeper into the brand's whisky. For adventurers, the distillery offers guided walks through the surrounding countryside. There is a wide range of tours on offer, as well as bespoke experiences for anyone looking for something a little more special. The Glenlivet's visitor's centre also houses a well-stocked shop, including distillery exclusives and bottle-your-own expressions.

Origins

The Glenlivet has been pivotal in the development of a legal Scottish single malt scene, braving the wrath and anger from illicit whisky distillers who were aggrieved at the move towards paying fees for licences as well as taxation on their products. This brave step was taken by George Smith, who had been an illicit distiller himself at

various farmsteads across what is now the Cairngorms National Park. Smith obtained a licence in 1824, a year after the Excise Act was passed in British Parliament. This makes The Glenlivet the first licensed distillery in Scotland.

The area around The Glenlivet was already famous for whisky-making, which contributed to the first visit of a British ruling monarch to Scotland for nearly a century. On King George IV's arrival in Edinburgh in 1822, he famously called for a dram of Glenlivet whisky. At the time, the suffix 'Glenlivet' was used by many distillers (such as Macallan-Glenlivet) but has been dropped in favour of simple, standalone distillery names, and to avoid confusion with The Glenlivet itself.

Smith consolidated his distilling to one site, Minmore Farm, and eventually moved it

further down the valley to take advantage of a better water source as demand grew.

After George Smith died in 1871, a succession of family members took over the business. His son John Gordon Smith first took over and in 1880 successfully applied for the sole use of the name 'Glenlivet'. George Smith's great-grandson, Captain Bill Smith is credited with accelerating the growth of the business and growing the fame of the brand internationally – he even persuaded the USA's Pullman train company to sell miniature bottles of The Glenlivet in its dining cars.

In the 1950s the distillery merged with Glen Grant (see page 160) and today it is owned by French drinks giant Pernod Ricard, as part of the Chivas Brothers family of distilleries which also includes Aberlour, Strathisla (see page 144) and Longmorn.

The Glenlivet Founder's Reserve

40% ABV

The nose begins with vanilla and freshly cut grass, evolving into fruity notes reminiscent of a Victoria sponge cake at a village summer fête. The palate is well-rounded, featuring light ginger beer, a hint of sarsaparilla and candied orange peel. The finish is light and delicate, with subtle hints of green herbs and fresh banana.

The Glenlivet 18 Years Old

40% ABV

The nose presents bold aromas of warm Cognac, rich oak and subtle hints of leather and suede. The palate builds on these notes, introducing cinnamon, cloves and a sweeter undertone of vanilla and toasted oak. This culminates in a finish that is both rich and oily.

34

The Dalmore

DALMORE · ALNESS · IV17 0UT · SCOTLAND

The Dalmore has become one of the most sought-after single malts around, thanks in part to being an unrivalled innovator of exceptionally old casks. Its new visitor's centre has been designed to reflect the whisky and its process.

The Dalmore distillery sits on the northern shores of the Cromarty Firth in the Scottish Highlands, near the town of Alness, about 20 miles north of Inverness. This coastal location provides an ideal environment for whisky production, with the cool, maritime climate playing an essential role in shaping the character of The Dalmore's whisky.

The Dalmore has a unique set up: the wash stills (the first in a double distillation) have usual flat tops and the spirit stills (the second in the distillation) are fitted with water jackets, adding reflux. This helps what should in theory be a big, oily spirit, to develop lighter notes and become a uniquely complex new make, crucial in creating The Dalmore's signature flavour profile, and a spirit that is famed for long maturation in different styles of casks such as sherry and port.

Strong relationships with sherry and port houses is something that has been cultivated under the tenure of Richard Paterson OBE, who has been the figurehead of the brand for over 60 years. The connection has also been invested in by master whisky maker, Greg Glass.

These relationships, particularly with the prestigious González Byass bodega in Jerez, Spain and the Graham's Port house in Porto, Portugal are key to the final product, as the casks have previously held rich sherries such as Oloroso and Pedro Ximénez, or tawny and vintage port wines. They impart deep, fruity, and spicy flavours to the whisky, such as raisins, chocolate and rich dried fruit.

In 2024, The Dalmore closed to invest heavily in a new visitor's centre and distillery, which opened in 2025. This purpose-built facility is simply stunning. Hidden away down by the Cromety Firth, and adjacent to an area of outstanding natural beauty, this new development is based on a traditional Scottish castle layout with a series of smaller, more intimate rooms. The view from the new distillery is worth the trip alone.

Origins

The Dalmore was founded in 1839 by Alexander Matheson, a successful entrepreneur who had made his fortune in Asia, mostly through the opium trade. Matheson was highly successful in business, and invested heavily in the surrounding area. (It is his historic castle that features in the UK and US versions of the hit TV show, *The Traitors*).

While Matheson established the distillery, it was operated from 1867 by the Mackenzie brothers who eventually bought Matheson out in 1891. Andrew and Charles Mackenzie played a pivotal role in The Dalmore's development, and their influence is still felt today; the family's connection to the Scottish Highlands and its history and heritage are intertwined with the distillery's identity. In recognition of the Mackenzie family history, The Dalmore adopted the clan's emblem – a 12-pointed royal stag – which remains a symbol of the brand to this day.

In 1960, the distillery merged with Whyte & Mackay, the famed blending company, in a move that expanded the brand's reach and allowed for greater investment in production and innovation. The 21st-century has seen The Dalmore rise to global prominence, particularly under the stewardship of master blender Richard Paterson OBE. Under Paterson's tenure, The Dalmore has released a range of premium expressions, including some of the most expensive whiskies in the world, such as The Dalmore 62 Years Old and The Dalmore 64 Trinitas.

The Dalmore 18 Years Old

43% ABV

The nose opens with rich mānuka honey and thick cherry jam, complemented by a touch of oak and warming spice. On the palate, sweet sugar puffs combine with walnuts, black cherries, and a hint of tart oak. The finish delivers toasted soda bread and a gentle touch of cloves.

The Dalmore 21 Years Old

43.8% ABV

This is a sherry lover's dream, with notes of old leather, cigar boxes and polished church pews on the nose. A balanced dryness is lifted by the distillery's spirit, bringing a sweet palate of red fruits, aged leather and cherry drops. The finish continues with these flavours, enhanced by a satisfying level of drying spices.

35

Glenmorangie

Famed for its tall 'giraffe-like' stills, Glenmorangie sits on the coast overlooking the Dornoch Firth, an enviable spot to make its unique single malt Scotch whisky.

The Glenmorangie distillery is something of an oddity. It is an historic place – it was founded in 1843 – with a name well known to whisky drinkers. Yet it is also a place of purpose and modern thinking. A former brewery, it feels old and new at the same time. This is in part thanks to a tall, modern glass building, which contrasts with the ancient stone of the original distillery buildings.

This new construction, 'The Lighthouse', is home to Glenmorangie's experimental stills and whisky development area. Off-limits to visitors, it is something of a talking point. It is also the physical embodiment of the distillery's vision: over the past two decades, Glenmorangie has introduced creative twists to its traditional single malt Scotch whisky. These changes have seen it stay consistently in the top-five-selling single malt Scotch whiskies globally for many years.

The rest of the site is a joy to visit. Located in the Northern Highlands, about an hour's drive north of Inverness, visitors arriving at Glenmorangie are ushered down a sloping road towards the sea – the distillery buildings are built deliberately along the right-hand side of the road.

The whisky starts with Glenmorangie's private water source, the Tarlogie Springs. This mineral-rich water is one of the key elements that gives Glenmorangie its signature flavour profile; it is one of only a handful of distilleries in Scotland to use a hard water source. Probably the most unique element of the Glenmorangie distillery, however, is its copper pot stills, the tallest in Scotland at over 8-m (26-ft) tall. They allow for only the lightest and purest vapours to ascend during distillation, leading to a spirit that is refined yet rich in delicate notes. These stills are said to be as tall as a giraffe, and the distillery uses the animal in much of its playful, colourful communication.

Maturation is an area of particular focus at Glenmorangie, which has pioneered the use of both secondary maturation ('finishing') and 'designer casks', which are those from specific, highly sought-after wine and spirits brands, such as chardonnay casks from the Sonoma-Cutrer winery in California's Sonoma Valley.

These adventures in maturation are the brainchild of Dr Bill Lumsden, the distillery's director of whisky creation (who also oversees the stocks and releases for Ardbeg – see page 112). Lumsden has pushed boundaries not just in maturation, but in whisky-making, too. His Signet series draws on barley that has been heavily roasted, or 'chocolate malt'. It is produced only once a year and, if you're lucky enough to be at the distillery when it is being distilled, the air fills with coffee and chocolate notes from the fermentation and distillation of this rich, roasted malted barley.

The distillery is also famed for its highly playful annual limited editions. Currently, this comes in the guise known as 'A Tale Of...', with releases such as A Tale of Tokyo – which is matured in Japanese Mizunara (see page 18) oak casks – and A Tale of Ice Cream – matured by Glenmorangie's master blender, Gillian Macdonald, and Dr Bill Lumsden, in high-vanillin casks.

Origins

Glenmorangie always seems to look forward, not back. It is not a brand that shouts loudly about its historic dates, choosing instead to focus on flavour, colour and innovation. But the distillery does have a rich history. It was founded in 1843 when William Matheson applied for a licence to distil on a small farm, though it would have been making whisky as early as 1703, illicitly.

Initially, it was a brewery that Matheson converted into a distillery to capitalize on the local barley and the mineral-rich waters from the nearby Tarlogie Springs. He

purchased former gin stills from London to make his spirit, with production starting in 1849.

Ownership of Glenmorangie changed several times throughout the 19th and 20th centuries. In 1918, the distillery was purchased by the Macdonald family, and their company Macdonald & Muir. Signs bearing this name can still be seen at the distillery today. Under the Macdonald family's guidance, Glenmorangie became a pioneering distillery, particularly in its use of wood management. In the 1980s, Glenmorangie was among the first distilleries to experiment with 'finishing'; ageing whisky in different types of casks, such as sherry and port, to enhance its flavour profile.

In 2004, Glenmorangie was acquired by French luxury goods company LVMH, where it sits in a small portfolio alongside only its sister distillery, Ardbeg, on the Isle of Islay.

Glenmorangie The Original 12 Years Old

40% ABV

The nose reveals delicate honey notes with a hint of lemon sherbet, petrichor, vanilla and fresh orange. The palate is beautifully balanced, showcasing oak, toasted malt and more orange reminiscent of crêpe suzette, alongside fresh lime zest and currants. The finish lingers with lavender and ripe peaches.

Glenmorangie Signet

46% ABV

The nose opens with rich aromas of freshly brewed coffee, cocoa nibs and warm cinnamon buns, accompanied by a robust cigar note. The palate is smooth yet structured, delivering flavours of black cherries, chocolate sauce and fine coffee. Sweet toasted marshmallow adds a delightful touch to the finish.

Highland Park

HOLM RD · KIRKWALL · KW15 1SU · SCOTLAND

One of Scotland's most northerly distilleries, Highland Park is an elemental site. It's located on the remote and rugged Orkney Islands, which rewards visitors with a warm welcome and one of the most beautiful and original distilleries that Scotland has to offer.

Highland Park produces an incredibly unique single malt that shows off the Islands of Orkney in a bottle. This distillery is a classic. Wrought iron gates with the brand name arched over the top welcome you in. The stone buildings, darkened with time and soot, appear as if they have been carved from the very cliffs that guard the island's shores. Moss clings to the weathered masonry, softening the sharp lines of the walls and roofs, blending the distillery seamlessly into its ancient surroundings, as though it has always been a part of this land. Highland Park is a bastion of tradition and stands stoic against the constant assault of the North Sea winds.

The pagoda roofs, unmistakable in their silhouettes, stand like watchful guardians over the distillery, their proud chimneys gently exhaling the faint scent of peat smoke into the salty air. The interior, which is just as atmospheric, is a maze of stone passageways, low-beamed ceilings and iron grates. In the still house, two sets of copper pot stills are always busy, seven days a week,

creating the delicate, floral spirit which is matured in both European and American oak casks. Unlike the cliffs of Orkney, the whisky from Highland Park is soft and, like the hills, it ages well. Highland Park has been seen in expressions of 40 years and older, still with life in it.

Tours are frequent, and include full access to the distillery plus a tasting, too. The silent season (see page 16) at Highland Park usually runs from July to September, so if you want to see the distillery in operation, avoid these months, or call ahead to check.

Origins

Highland Park is as much a part of Orkney as the stones of Stenness or the cliffs of Yesnaby. Today, as it closes in on 250 years of operation, it stands as a monument to the craftsmanship of generations and to the resilient spirit of these remote islands and their people.

The date on the gates that guard Highland Park proclaim that it was founded in

1798, making it one of the oldest working distilleries in Scotland. It was established by Magnus Eunson, a local church officer and notorious smuggler, and stories abound about his ability to hide his wares from the local government officials. One story claims that Eunson hid a cask under a blanket and passed it off as a coffin to avoid being caught. Eventually, his distilling operation gained attention and Highland Park became a legal entity in the early-19th century.

In 1826, the distillery was officially licenced and its reputation for producing high-quality whisky grew steadily over the following decades. In the late-19th century, Highland Park was acquired by Robert Borwick, a prominent merchant who expanded production and invested in the distillery's facilities. In the 1930s, Highland Park was purchased by Highland Distillers, now part of the Edrington Group and owner of The Macallan (see page 156). Today, Highland Park is still part of the company's portfolio.

Housed on the outskirts of Kirkwall, Orkney's capital, the distillery's unique geographic location plays an essential role in shaping the character of Highland Park whisky – the peat is sourced from Hobbister Moor, 7 miles west of the distillery. One of the island's calling cards is the lack of trees, which in turn creates a peat style that, when burnt to dry the malted barley, leaves a distinctly floral smoke style in the resulting spirit.

Highland Park 12 Years Old

40% ABV

The nose opens with a rich blend of toffee, vanilla and soft sugars, complemented by poached pears, honey and a touch of floral smoke. The smooth palate reveals chopped walnuts, candied lemon rind and honey, with subtle hints of fennel seed and wood smoke. The finish is medium-light with a gentle sweetness.

Highland Park 18 Years Old

43% ABV

The nose presents smoked cherry drops, crème anglaise, cinnamon and a hint of salt. On the palate, it begins with creamy Black Forest gateaux, transitioning into stone fruits, smoke, forest floor notes, iodine and dark chocolate. The finish is a harmonious blend of fruity and smoky elements.

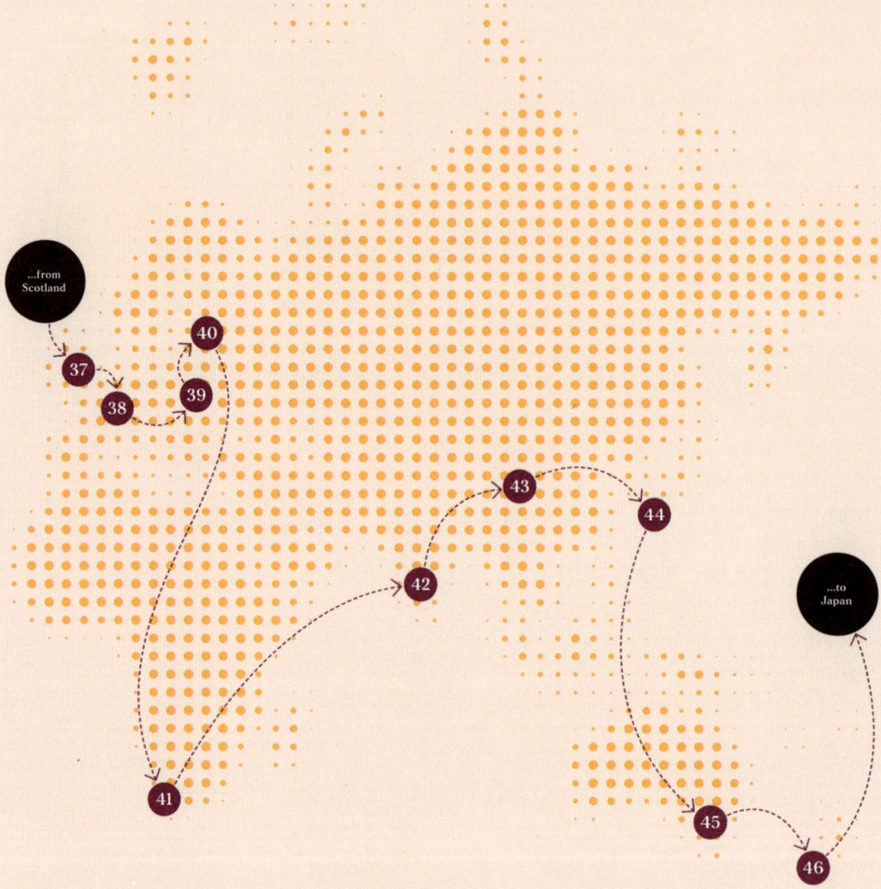
...from Scotland
37
38
39
40
41
42
43
44
45
46
...to Japan

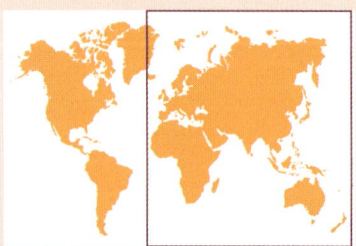

Rest of the World

A dispatch from the Rest of the World

The world of whisky-making has historically been the domain of only a few, select countries. If 'whisky' were to be a music festival, the headliner would surely be Scotch whisky, with the supporting acts from Ireland, America (in the form of bourbon) and the century-old 'newcomer' to the scene, Japan. Sure, Canadian whisky would feature high on the bill, but its mixable, drinkable, massive-brand-driven approach holds it back in reputation slightly, if not in sales.

Yet, as anyone who has been to a good music festival will tell you, the real discoveries are to be had in the fringe tents, with the up-and-coming artists. For whisky, the 'Rest of the World' category is that very place.

The rise in global whisky production is unprecedented. At no time in history have more whisky distilleries been recorded in more countries. From Canada to China, Texas to Taiwan, whisky seems to be everywhere, and this is evidenced in the Rest of World section in this book.

There is no one place where you could say the trend of 'worldwide whisky' production started. Japan was the trendsetter, but its scene is a century old and is now an established 'terroir' in its own right. You could look to Amrut, from India (see page 204) which launched its single malt in 2004

in Glasgow, no less, or even to Taiwanese entry Kavalan (see page 212) that opened in 2005 for grabbing the single malt spotlight from Scotch. But there is no real one brand or distiller whom we could call the genesis of the scene.

Today, large numbers of start-ups are adopting the traditional Scottish way of making single malt (see Cotswolds on page 184), but this is not always true. Domaine des Hautes Glaces (see page 188) from France is basing all its products on different grains such as oats, wheat and spelt, as well as barley. Starward distillery (page 216) in Melbourne, meanwhile, matures in an environment where it loses water, not alcohol, from its casks so it must fill at a lower ABV to others and watch it rise over time.

This legion of new distilleries dotted around the world is just picking up on the idea of welcoming visitors. Not because they're against the idea, but simply because whisky fans are now wanting to visit. They want to see, smell, taste and understand the whisky they love made in Taiwan, England or South Africa – and the distillers want to showcase their wares.

As such we are starting to see visitor's centres open up at these new-world distilleries. Not only that, tours are seen as profit-drivers, a way to fill up one side of the spreadsheet while the other is leaking with

grain and barrel purchases, electricity and gas bills, staff wages, marketing and travel expenses, not to mention a decade spent waiting to get all those outgoings back in.

However, these distilleries, pushing a new frontier, are often just that: new. Of the featured distilleries in this Rest of the World section, just one was making single malt pre-2000 (James Sedgewick, since 1990). As such, some of their 'origin' stories have been woven into the wider distillery profile, showing off a more of a complete biography of the place, the people and the process, for a selection of these sophomore sites.

This is all very exciting for the whisky pilgrim, the nomad taster who wants to explore and be educated. Whisky does not carry a passport, nor does it wave a flag. It is a global citizen, and at no time in history has this ever been more true – and it comes at a time when greater choice and diversity is needed.

Cotswolds

PHILLIP'S FIELD · WHICHFORD ROAD · STOURTON · CV36 5EX · ENGLAND

Not many whisky producers are located in a designated Area of Outstanding National Beauty. The Cotswolds distillery, the largest maker in England, has made this place its own. And its visitor experience reflects the location's stunning surroundings.

The picturesque Cotswolds region of England has fast become a hotbed for those looking to get away from London's fast pace, or for tourists wanting to experience an old, quaint corner of England. The honey-coloured stone and quiet villages are postcard perfect, and the region has fast become the poster child for England's natural beauty.

So what better place to build a whisky distillery? It is rural, has great water, fantastic barley and a wonderful reputation for quality hospitality (Soho Farmhouse, Estelle Manor and Daylesford, to name a few). And this was the vision of founder Daniel Szor when he opened the distillery in 2014. Today, among the rolling Cotswold hills, the distillery feels less like a modern business and more like a natural extension of the landscape itself.

At first, the distillery was making a Cotswold-led gin (think lavender and freshly cut grass), but all the while, in the background, there was single malt whisky being made. As the gin sold, and the brand grew, so did the stocks of maturing whisky, reflected today in its range.

Production-wise, this is another distillery from the canon of new-to-world producers (see also Kavalan, page 212) that has the late Dr Jim Swan to thank. The consultant distiller has helped numerous new single malt whisky distillers in their set-up, production flow and maturation (he favoured a complex but wonderful 'de-char, re-char' cask style) and the distillery is home to four copper pot stills with a capacity of around 500,000 litres (110,000 gallons) per year. All the barley used for the single malt is grown locally.

The distillery has set high standards for quality and sustainability, and has become the largest producer of single malt in England. Its Cotswolds Single Malt has garnered acclaim for its rich fruit and balanced character. The whisky is aged in American oak barrels, and each batch showcases the distillery's commitment to ensuring English whisky has a strong future.

What sets the Cotswolds distillery apart is its strong emphasis on sustainability. The distillery aims to reduce its carbon footprint and minimize waste by using local ingredients and embracing eco-friendly practices. It feeds its spent grains to local cattle, furthering its commitment to the environment and community.

The distillery, in such a popular tourist area, is set up well for visitors. You can choose between a number of different tour options, including a whisky blending masterclass. And for anyone who has a palate tired of whisky, there are gin tours, too. The distillery has also been awarded a Gold Medal by VisitEngland for its experiences, as well as Travellers' Choice Awards from TripAdvisor.

Origins

The Cotswolds distillery was founded in 2014 as the vision to blend the rich agricultural traditions of the Cotswolds with the craft of distilling by founder, Daniel Szor. An American financier turned whisky enthusiast, Szor was captivated by the beauty of the Cotswolds and its potential for creating fine spirits, inspired by the success of small-scale distilleries in Scotland.

Based in the village of Stourton, Warwickshire, within the rolling hills of the Cotswolds, the distillery was one of the first of its kind in England, marking a departure from the area's agricultural roots to embrace the world of craft distilling. Szor's vision was to create high-quality, small-batch spirits using locally sourced ingredients, with an emphasis on authenticity and craftsmanship. The distillery's first creation, Cotswolds Dry Gin, focused on the use of local lavender and other native herbs. However, Szor's true passion was whisky and, in 2017, the distillery released its inaugural Cotswolds Single Malt, made from 100 per cent locally grown barley. In 2022, the distillery expanded by building an entirely new area to house its whisky production and allow for greater production capacity.

Cotswolds Signature Single Malt

46% ABV

The nose is rich and oily, with a lingering hint of spice, candied orange peel, lavender, oak and a subtle touch of white wine. The palate brings together figs, dates and a hint of damson jam and quince. The finish is warm, with malt and gentle spices.

Cotswolds Founder's Choice Single Malt

59.1% ABV

Fruity and floral notes form a delightful mix on the nose, with coconut, pineapple, vanilla and pear. On the palate, flavours of marshmallows over hot chocolate are accompanied by vintage leather and the warmth of a copper mug. The finish is long and spiced, leaving a lasting impression.

38

Domaine des Hautes Glaces

185 RTE DU COL · 38710 CORNILLON-EN-TRIÈVES · FRANCE

A pioneering French whisky distillery located high in the French Alps, Domaine des Hautes Glaces has a distinct focus on grains and terroir, distilling not just whisky, but the land on which it sits.

All whisky distilleries are a product of their place. You only have to visit the Isle of Islay in Scotland to see this; how the peat bogs have left their fragrant aroma on the whisky the island makes. The same can be said for expertise. The reason the American whiskey industry exists is because of the skills brought to the frontier farmsteads by foreign immigrants. Skills that had been honed in Celtic countries such as Ireland and Scotland, where distilling from grain was woven into the agricultural practices of the day, and were a real reflection of the land in which they were built.

Take this ideal, that the grains and the land are of huge importance, along with skills honed over time, and place it in the bucolic French Alps. The result: the Domaine des Hautes Glaces disitllery and its whiskies.

This French whisky distillery – which sits at 900m (2,953ft) in Trièves, in the outer reaches of the Isère, Drôme and Hautes-Alpes departments of France – embodies a fusion of terroir-driven craftsmanship, organic farming and a deep respect for sustainability. These are the defining features of Domaine des Hautes Glaces and, unlike conventional distilleries that often rely on industrially sourced grains, here the distillery cultivates its own crops using 19 different farmers to grow barley, rye, spelt and oats, all without chemical pesticides or synthetic fertilizers.

This organic approach not only enhances the quality of the whisky but also preserves soil health and biodiversity. The distillery operates using renewable energy sources, including hydroelectric power from nearby mountain streams and solar energy, reducing its carbon footprint significantly.

The water used in whisky production is locally sourced from the surrounding mountain streams, with the entire process, from field to bottle, carried out with a philosophy of minimal intervention, allowing nature to dictate the nuances of each batch.

Long fermentation times are employed, using local wild yeast in wooden vats, rather than stainless steel, further contributing to the development of complex flavours, with some of the grains smoked over chestnut to

add yet another layer of flavour. Distillation is carried out on traditional French Charentais-style stills (more commonly seen in the distillation of Cognac), which are wood fired. Maturation is across a number of different cask types, including French oak barrels sourced from wine and Cognac producers.

The distillery welcomes visitors with a series of different offerings – from private tours and tasting sessions in their cellar, to foodie workshops, artist residencies, exhibitions, screenings and concerts – making this a site where whisky is not just distilled, but creativity is also cultivated.

Seasonal opening is operated (the 'low season' is October to April, the 'high season' May to September), so do check when tours will run before visiting. Several themed workshops are also held throughout the

year, including cheese and whisky pairings, and a gourmet workshop with food prepared by local artisans.

Origins

Founded in 2009 by Frédéric Revol, Domaine des Hautes Glaces was conceived as an ambitious experiment: to prove that whisky could be entirely terroir-driven, much like fine wine. Inspired by the traditions of French viticulture, the distillery sources its grains – barley, rye, oats and wheat – from organic farms, ensuring a unique and authentic representation of its Alpine surroundings in every bottle.

Revol, an agronomist by training, envisioned a self-sufficient whisky estate that upheld the values of biodynamic farming, renewable energy use, and minimal environmental impact. From the beginning, this distillery has championed the idea that whisky should reflect the land it comes from, capturing the essence of its raw materials and the climate in which they are grown.

In 2017 it was announced that the French drinks company Rémy Cointreau had acquired the business, adding to a portfolio that includes the Bruichladdich Scotch whisky distillery on Islay, as well as Rémy Martin and Louis XIII cognacs and Cointreau liqueur.

Hautes Glaces Indigene Single Malt Whisky

44% ABV

The nose opens with delicate oak spices, backed with summer fruit, white peaches and green apples. There is a hint of marzipan with some sugar sweetness. On the palate, a there is a lychee note which is underpinned by malt and fresh white flowers. Some light peppery notes and a hint of peach and pear. The finish has lemon rind and white chocolate, with some notes of crème brûlée at the end.

Hautes Glaces Vulson Single Malt Whisky

43% ABV

This expression is triple-distilled and gives a lovely light aroma of freshly baked bread, lavender, lily of the valley and lemon peel on the nose. It is complex despite its lightness. The palate delivers deeper flavours of earthy liquorice, more lemon and fresh green apples. Slightly tart with a hint of pine and some white pepper. The finish has light green tea notes and some more white pepper, with an enduring note of lavender.

39

Slyrs

BAYRISCHZELLER STRASSE 13 · 83727 SCHLIERSEE · GERMANY

There are few places in Bavaria where you can feel so keenly the romance of the mountains, the charm of tradition and the pleasure of fine craftsmanship as at Slyrs distillery. Hidden in the foothills of the Bavarian Alps, not far from the tranquil waters of Lake Schliersee, it is a place where whisky is not merely made but nurtured by the crisp, alpine air.

The journey to the Slyrs distillery alone is worth the trip. Leaving behind the bustle of Munich, the road winds southward into a landscape of rolling meadows and verdant forests, with the peaks of the Alps rising ever closer. Then, suddenly, nestled amid storybook scenery, the distillery appears: a cluster of low wooden buildings, their flower-laden balconies lending a homely charm. The name Slyrs (pronounced 'Schliers') is derived from a monastery founded in 779, and is a proud reminder of the distillery's roots, anchoring it firmly in Bavarian heritage.

Stepping inside, one is greeted by the warmth of wood-panelled interiors, where the inviting scent of ageing whisky drifts through the air. Visitors have a choice of a self-guided tour (around 40 minutes long) or joining a guided tour that reveals the secrets of the craft, from mashing to maturation, culminating in the barrel hall, where golden spirit rests in quiet contemplation. In a modern, lounge-like tasting room, one may

sip and savour, or even, in the company of fellow enthusiasts, blend your own whisky liqueur in a whisky workshop open to five or more guests.

Yet Slyrs is more than just a whisky distillery; it is a gathering place, a celebration of Bavarian life. Whisky dinners, held in convivial style, marry the finest local produce with carefully chosen drams, while, on summer evenings, whisky-barbecues on the sun terrace provide a setting as memorable as the whisky itself. Music drifts through the air at seasonal festivals, and cigars, for those so inclined, are paired with whisky in a manner befitting the leisurely pace of the mountains.

Distilling has been in the blood of the team here since 1928, with whisky-making starting in 1999. With over a quarter of a century of whisky-making expertise behind them, the liquid shows real evidence, in their range of well made, and well matured whiskies, of a complete understanding of what makes distilled spirits great.

Since its launch, Slyrs has earned its place among Europe's most intriguing whisky producers, built on crisp water drawn from the Bannwald spring in the Schliersee Alps as pure as the mountain air, and the barley, grown close to Munich, which imparts the flavour of the land into every bottle. A visit here to see the process, taste the whisky and experience the local culture will create memories that linger long after the last drop.

Origins

The story of Slyrs began in 1999 when trained brewer Florian Stetter, inspired by a visit to Scotland, set out to create a Bavarian single malt that could stand alongside the greats. Unlike the centuries-old Scottish distilleries, Slyrs is a relatively young player in the whisky world, but it has quickly earned a reputation for quality and innovation.

To understand the true history of Slyrs, you must go further back to 1928, when Stetter's grandparents laid the foundations of the Lantenhammer distillery just 15 minutes drive away, in Hausham. The Lantenhammer distillery, known for its fruit brandies crafted with the care and patience of artisans who understood the secrets of distillation, was the place where Florian Stetter started to work in 1985, a grandson inheriting not just a business but a legacy. Yet, his vision went beyond tradition; he saw the potential for something bold, something new, and it is where he first distilled what is today Slyrs whisky.

In 2002, the first bottles of whisky with Slyrs on the label were on sale. The dream soon outgrew its birthplace. In 2007, a dedicated whisky distillery was built in

Neuhaus am Schliersee, a place chosen for its pure mountain water and crisp alpine air. Here, under the watchful eye of Hans Kemenater – who had joined Lantenhammer in 1999 and brought with him a craftsman's touch – the spirit of Slyrs matured. Kemenater took up the mantle of production manager, guiding the fledgling whisky with the steady hand of experience.

Today, the distillery's core whisky is made using locally grown, unsmoked malt (although it also offers a Mountain Edition, the malt of which is smoked with beech wood, giving a unique, rich and textured spirit, and Bavarian Peat, that is smoked with peat). The distillery employs two 5,000-litre (1,100-gallon) wash stills and a 6,000-litre (1,320-gallon) spirit still, the whisky is then matured predominantly in virgin American white oak casks, with the exception of the Rye whisky, that is matured in ex-bourbon casks. Slyrs offers a range of expressions including a 12-year-old single malt and an 18-year-old single malt. It also produces a rye whisky using locally grown cereal, and a fully peated offering, Bavarian Peat, too.

SLYRS Single Malt Whisky Classic

43% ABV

A gentle, warming note to the nose, and an array of summer fruits, backed with vanilla spice and some cloves. On the palate there is a note of tropical fruit, cinnamon, marzipan, cream and gingerbread. The finish is sweet, buttery and beautifully spiced with a slight savory, earthiness at the end.

SLYRS Bavarian Rye Whisky

41% ABV

The nose presents a rustic array of autumnal aromas: fresh rye bread, with earthy, grassy undertones. There's also a soft sweetness, with notes of caramel and red apple. The palate gives ginger, toffee apple, anise and rye spice, backed with freshly baked doughnuts. The whisky's texture is slightly chewy, giving the impression of freshly baked rye bread, with a long finish of lingering peppery warmth.

40

Stauning

STAUNINGVEJ 38 · 6900 SKJERN · DENMARK

Denmark might not seem like the obvious place to make whisky, and that is exactly what gives Stauning a point of difference. The team behind it approached the distillery's set up in a very unique way with brilliant results. And the stunning design is a feast for the eyes, too.

What sets Stauning whisky apart is its dedication to using 100 per cent Danish-sourced ingredients. All the barley and rye used in production are grown locally, and the water comes from a nearby spring. Its commitment to traditional methods is evident in its malting process, too, which is done onsite using floor malting (see page 17). It also dries the malt using Danish peat and heather, as well as seaweed and pine, giving the whisky a distinctive regional flavour. Stauning produces both malt and rye whisky, although its Stauning Rye, made from local grains and with a rich, spicy character, is one of its signature expressions.

The distillery's design-led visitor's centre sits beautifully within the rugged natural surroundings of West Jutland, where North Sea winds and Danish weather play a subtle role in the whisky's maturation. The distillery is open to the public, and you can tour the facility, watch the floor malting process, and see the copper stills in action.

Origins

Located in a remote part of western Denmark, Stauning has quickly earned a place among the most innovative and distinctive whisky producers in the world. Founded in 2005 by a group of nine friends with a shared passion for whisky, but with no experience of making it, the team took

an unusual route to solving the problems of distilling a spirit. The nine founders came from diverse professional backgrounds, ranging from doctors to pilots to chefs, but were united by a love of whisky. Their dream was to create Danish whisky with local ingredients and craftsmanship, using traditional production methods that were adapted to the Danish environment. Their initial efforts were modest, operating out of a small farm with handmade equipment and experimenting with local grains and techniques. The results, however, were quite surprising and early experiments, particularly their smoked whiskies, which used Danish peat and heather, garnered critical acclaim. These early endorsements encouraged the team to pursue their vision more seriously and operations expanded.

In 2015, Stauning caught the attention of Johnnie Walker owner Diageo, who invested an astonishing £10 million, allowing for an entirely new development to be built. This was not about changing the crafted style, but simply replicating it over and over. The construction was almost a 'cut and paste' job of the existing distillery, multiple times. Today the distillery is home to 24 small copper stills, all direct fired, with floor malting, too.

Stauning Bastard

46.3% ABV

The nose is dominated by oak and smoke, layered with chopped pine and subtle hints of basil. On the palate, earthy tones blend with polished pine and rich peat smoke, leading to a well-rounded finish, with delicate traces of burning moss and a touch of mint.

Stauning HØST

40.5% ABV

Rye spice combines with sugary tea, honey and freshly cut grass on the nose of this whisky. The palate mirrors this, although it is softened by creamy vanilla notes and a hint of gooseberry. The finish delivers strong grape Kool-Aid, balanced with rye spice and grassy undertones.

41

James Sedgwick

79 STOKERY RD · WELLINGTON · 7654 · SOUTH AFRICA

The James Sedgwick distillery in South Africa is an important place. While whisky distilleries are popping up all over the world, there are precious few in Africa. The James Sedgwick distillery is a trailblazer and should be on everyone's radar when visiting Cape Town.

Located in the small town of Wellington, a 45-minute drive from Cape Town, James Sedgwick distillery (JSD) is home to some of South Africa's most renowned whiskies, including the award-winning Three Ships and Bain's Cape Mountain, both of which are utterly fantastic. A trip to this distillery is not just a lesson in whisky production, but an immersion in South Africa's rich history and natural beauty.

JSD was established as a distillery in 1886, but back then it made brandy. It was named after Captain James Sedgwick, a British mariner and adventurer who settled in South Africa and left his mark on the country's spirits industry. The site began making whisky in 1999 and today it stands as a pioneer in South Africa's production of the spirit. And credit is due to ex-England cricket player, Andy Watts, who is also the former master distiller at JSD. Watts, who grew up in Yorkshire, would spend half his year in England and the other half in South Africa earning a living with bat and ball. After his retirement from sport, he moved

into whisky-making. And what whisky-making it was! Watts has played a pivotal role in elevating the status of South African whisky and, under his leadership, the country's whisky has gained recognition on the international stage.

A visit to the James Sedgwick distillery starts with a guided tour that takes you through the entire whisky-making process. Guests are welcomed with a brief history of the distillery, an introduction to the whisky brands it produces, and a welcome drink. As you tour the distillery, you'll learn about the meticulous process of mashing, fermentation, distillation and maturation that turns South African grains into premium whisky. These intimate tours take place on select Fridays and Saturdays for just 20 guests at a time. Each trip concludes with a whisky tasting and the chance to purchase the bottles of your choice. Booking is essential.

The distillery's location in Wellington, nestled at the foot of the Hawequa Mountains, adds to the charm of the experience. The surrounding vineyards and rugged landscapes create a serene atmosphere that complements the rich history and craft of the distillery. It's an ideal spot for visitors who want to explore the scenic beauty of South Africa's Western Cape while indulging in world-class whisky.

Three Ships 12 Years Old

46.3% ABV

The nose opens with a prominent wine character, accompanied by cherry drops, cinnamon candies and a hint of orange zest. On the palate, bold blood orange flavours emerge, followed by sweetened tea and a touch of vermouth. The finish is rich and fruity, with a gentle hint of spice.

Bain's Cape Mountain

40% ABV

The nose leads with a blend of spices, vanilla and a subtle note of pineapple skin. The palate reveals layers of sweet grain, followed by cooking apples, nutmeg and cedar wood. The finish brings more cedar wood, oak spice and a faint touch of green chilli.

42

Amrut

41/1 · 72ND CROSS RD · BENGALURU · KARNATAKA 560010 · INDIA

When it came to sales, Amrut distillery in India took a completely different route when it launched its single malt in 2004. Far from focusing on its home market (India is a huge whisky-loving country), it decided that export was key. The decision has put the distillery in a good position, and Amrut is now a household name in the world of whisky.

Amrut, which is based in Bengaluru (Bangalore), Karnataka, was the first distillery to produce an Indian single malt whisky, which now competes with some of the best in the world. The distillery was established in 1948 by the Jagdale Group, just a year after India gained independence. Initially, the distillery focused on producing rum, brandy and other spirits such as local whisky or IMFL (Indian-made foreign liquor, made mostly using molasses so not able to be sold as whisky elsewhere in the world). These were widely consumed across India. However, in 2001, Amrut shifted its attention to crafting whisky, marking a turning point for India's position in the global whisky market.

It wasn't until 2004 that Amrut released its first single malt whisky (appropriately named Amrut Single Malt), to much fanfare and critical acclaim. And where best to launch your new single malt, but Scotland? Amrut's whisky was first introduced in Glasgow and quickly gained a reputation

for its quality, challenging the traditional dominance of Scottish and Irish whiskies on the global stage. Today, Amrut is known for producing premium single malts that have earned awards from whisky connoisseurs and competitions around the world.

A visit to the Amrut distillery shows off one of the most important elements of its whisky-making – a brewing process that uses Indian-grown barley and Himalayan spring water to create the foundation of these single malt whiskies. For some of the expressions, Amrut cuts its own barley with some peated stocks from Scotland. Fermentation time often exceeds 140 hours.

The distillery features eight copper pot stills, using double distillation, and occasionally it experiments with triple distillation. One of the most fascinating aspects of the Amrut distillery is the maturation warehouses, where rows upon rows of casks are stored to age, at 915m (3,000ft) above sea level. The influence of the tropical climate is evident

in the maturation process, as the higher evaporation rate enhances the interaction between the whisky and the wood. This rapid maturation comes at a cost: the 'angels' share' here sits at around 10 to 12 per cent every year, resulting in deeply complex and richly flavoured whiskies.

Amrut's whiskies have been widely credited for starting a trend of single malt whisky-making in India. Today there are 11 other single malt distillers currently in production in the country, with a host of others either being built or in the planning stages. The home market holds single malt in high regard, and in 2023 half of all single malt consumed in India was produced domestically. This highlights that the category, which Amrut helped to forge, is one to keep a keen eye on for any fans of world whisky.

Indian single malt is no longer an outlier on the shelves of whisky shops worldwide, and now represents serious, high quality, well-made whisky with Amrut at the forefront.

Amrut Single Malt

46% ABV

The nose opens with green cooking apples dusted with cinnamon, followed by creamy custard and delicate yellow floral notes. On the palate, the flavours are light and balanced, with fresh green apples, almond nuttiness and a touch of spice. The finish brings back the custard and enhances the spice.

Amrut Fusion Single Malt

50% ABV

A rich vanilla aroma dominates the nose with hints of lemongrass and ginger ale. The palate is smooth and inviting, offering honeyed sweetness, vanilla ice cream and crisp green apples. The finish delivers a zesty twist of lime pickle and fresh green grass, rounding off the experience.

43

The Chuan

DAYI COUNTY · CHENGDU · SICHUAN · 611335 · CHINA

If great whisky-making is all about resources, both human and agricultural, then there is no reason why China should not make exceptional whisky. And, with heavy investment from some of the world's biggest drinks companies, loaded with history and experience, the race is on for China's own whisky-making scene. The Chuan distillery from French distilling giant Pernod Ricard represents a bold new chapter for the country's spirit scene.

The Chuan distillery, nestled amid the mist-shrouded southern foothills of the Emei mountains and fertile plains of this ancient land, is both a symbol of China's modern whisky ambitions and a tribute to the country's rich cultural heritage. The site is located in China's Sichuan, a province better known for its fiery cuisines and rolling tea plantations than its whisky. Yet here, amid the towering peaks and sparkling streams, beside bamboo groves and peppercorn trees, The Chuan distillery has found a home overlooked only by the imposing and spiritual Mount Emei, a Unesco World Heritage Site. The location was no accident. The founders, inspired by whisky's growing global appeal, had scoured China for the perfect spot, eventually settling on this mountainous region for its pure, mineral-rich water and temperate climate.

The story of The Chuan is not merely one of whisky production; it is one of convergence – the blend of Chinese philosophy and Western technique. The distillery is a testament to this vision: a modern yet simple structure, the site hums with the quiet industry of craftsmanship. Opened in 2021, it was designed by Shanghai-based architects Neri & Hu at a cost of 1.5 billion Chinese Yen (£7.5 million).

Some of the malt for The Chuan whisky is sourced locally. Sichuan barley, golden and thick, grown in the rich soil of the province's plains, is harvested once a year. Fermentation times are long at 90 hours. The distillation happens on two traditional copper pot stills made by Forsyths in Scotland. But it is the water that is most prized, drawn from the pure mountain springs that flow from the highlands. Hot, humid summers and cool, misty winters create an atmosphere that quickens the ageing process.

The Chuan ages its whisky in a variety of oak barrels – some from America, others

The Chuan
Pure Malt

40% ABV

A nose of soft floral and fruity aromas, including ripe apple and pear, mingling with light honey. On the palate, it offers smooth notes of malted barley, vanilla and a touch of toasted oak, with a subtle layer of sweet spice. The finish is gentle and lingering, with hints of dried fruit and a whisper of oak spice.

from France and a few from the forests of China itself, using Danling oak, the rare Quercus mongolica sourced from the eastern side of the slope of Changbai mountain. Each barrel breathes life into the whisky, imparting flavours of vanilla, dark fruit and the soft spice of the wood. As yet, there is no official '100 per cent The Chuan' whisky, due to the youthful nature of the distillery, but there is a bottling which brings together existing Scotch whisky and some of the younger Chinese single malt.

In 2023, a visitor's centre opened at the distillery and features two main spaces: the circle and the square. The 'circle' is designed as a tasting-experience building, hidden partly underground with five subterranean tasting rooms and a central, rain-like water feature. The 'square' features a restaurant and bar.

44

Kavalan

The Kavalan distillery has made an indelible mark on the global single malt scene since it opened in 2005. A pioneer of world whisky, it has proved that award-winning whisky can be made anywhere in the world. Its visitor experience is also first class, and puts a spotlight on this quite wonderful distillery.

Kavalan's rapid rise to fame is down to one thing: great whisky. In fact, its releases have become known for their consistency with the distillery set up to produce the highest quality spirit possible. One of just two Taiwanese whisky distilleries (at the time of writing), Kavalan is located in the northeastern part of Taiwan in Yilan County, around an hour's drive from the country's capital of Taipei. The distillery is another by the late Dr Jim Swan (see page 184), a man instrumental in helping a new wave of single malt distilleries get up and running quickly.

The first spirit ran from the copper pot stills at Kavalan on 11 March 2006, at 3:30pm. No one knew how well this spirit would go on to mature and a decade later the distillery had expanded to become, at that time, one of the top ten biggest malt distilleries in the world. Quite the meteoric rise. The distillery, operated by the King Car Group, a large Taiwanese food and beverage conglomerate owned by businessman T T Lee, is named after the indigenous Kavalan

people, reflecting its deep connection to the local culture and environment. Inspired by his love for whisky and driven by the belief that Taiwan's unique climate could create distinctive whisky, Lee set out to establish a state-of-the-art distillery in Yilan County.

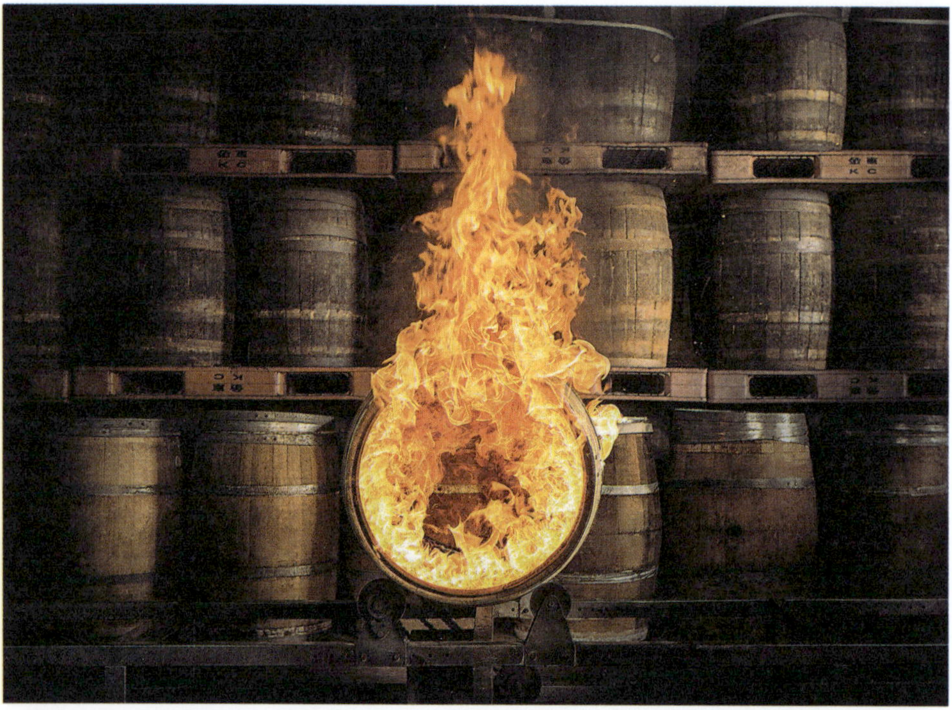

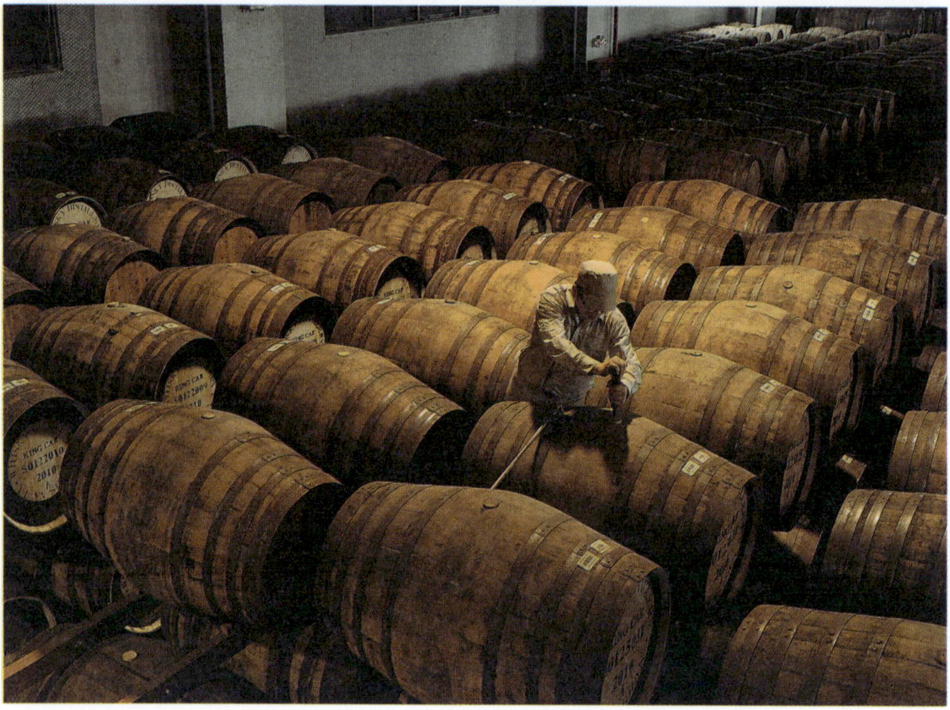
KING CAR

The distillery's location was carefully chosen for its pristine environment and abundant natural resources. Yilan's clean air, pure spring water from Snow Mountain, and its subtropical climate play a crucial role in shaping Kavalan's whisky. While the spirit traditionally matures in cooler climates, Kavalan benefits from Taiwan's hot and humid weather, which accelerates the ageing process and leads to rich, complex flavours in a shorter time frame. The temperatures for maturation can reach above 40°C (104°F), and the 'angels' share' can reach well beyond 10 per cent per annum. On top of this, there are earthquakes, too.

Kavalan's production process, built around Swan's specification and under the guidance of Ian Chang (now a consultant distiller), uses ten pairs of traditional copper pot stills and carefully selects its barrels with a focus on high-quality casks such as American oak, sherry, bourbon and wine casks. The influence of these on Kavalan's whisky is profound, contributing to its signature depth and complexity. It was these whiskies, released under the Solist banner, often as single casks, which laid the foundations for Kavalan's success.

The distillery has a fantastic visitor's centre, and welcomes more than a million people a year. Currently, it offers tours in Chinese, English and Japanese. The distillery is open every day and all year round (note, on Lunar New Year's Eve the venue closes early). Each tour session is about 30 minutes and covers the original distillery and production process, plus its 'Spirit Castle' tasting area.

Kavalan Select No.1

40% ABV

The nose reveals rich toffee notes intertwined with a touch of Armagnac-like grape sweetness and a hint of lime pickle. On the palate, a sweet barbecue sauce leads the way, evolving into earthy undertones and freshly chopped oak, with oak spices lingering into the finish.

Kavalan Classic Single Malt

40% ABV

The aroma opens with the comforting scent of ginger cake, complemented by a dash of vanilla spices and the essence of vintage furniture. The palate showcases vibrant mandarin and orange notes, enhanced by fresh lime zest and a subtle hint of oak. As the finish unfolds, oak spices emerge alongside tropical hints of mango and passion fruit, creating a delightful experience.

45

Starward

50 BERTIE ST · PORT MELBOURNE VIC 3207 · AUSTRALIA

Few distillers in the world of whisky set out to disrupt the norm, and those that do often fail quickly in an industry that can be stuck in its ways. Starward, however, achieved just this, and the Melbourne-based distillery's whiskies have since taken the world by storm.

Starward's founder David Vitale had a dream to make whisky in Melbourne and, in 2013, the first bottle from his distillery hit the shelves, deliberately set at a price that was designed for drinking. Vitale's aim was simple: create a modern Australian whisky that reflects the country's unique culture and environment, as well as the city it calls home. And with its bold, almost audacious spirit, Starward has captured the essence of

this vibrant metropolis, and amazing, vast country.

Starward was born out of Vitale's vision to create a whisky that could stand out globally but still maintain a deep connection to Australia. Melbourne, with its dynamic weather, and vibrant food and drink scene, offered the perfect environment for such a project. The city's 'four seasons in one day', as natives Crowded House sang, accelerates the maturation process, enabling Starward to achieve complex and rich flavours in a shorter time than many traditional whiskies.

Starward uses 100 per cent Australian ingredients in its production process. The barley used is sourced from Australian farms, and the water comes from local sources. For maturation, Vitale was inspired by Melbourne's thriving wine culture and decided to age Starward whiskies in Australian red wine barrels. This bold choice sets Starward apart from many distilleries that rely on bourbon or sherry casks for ageing. By embracing local wine barrels, Vitale not only created a whisky

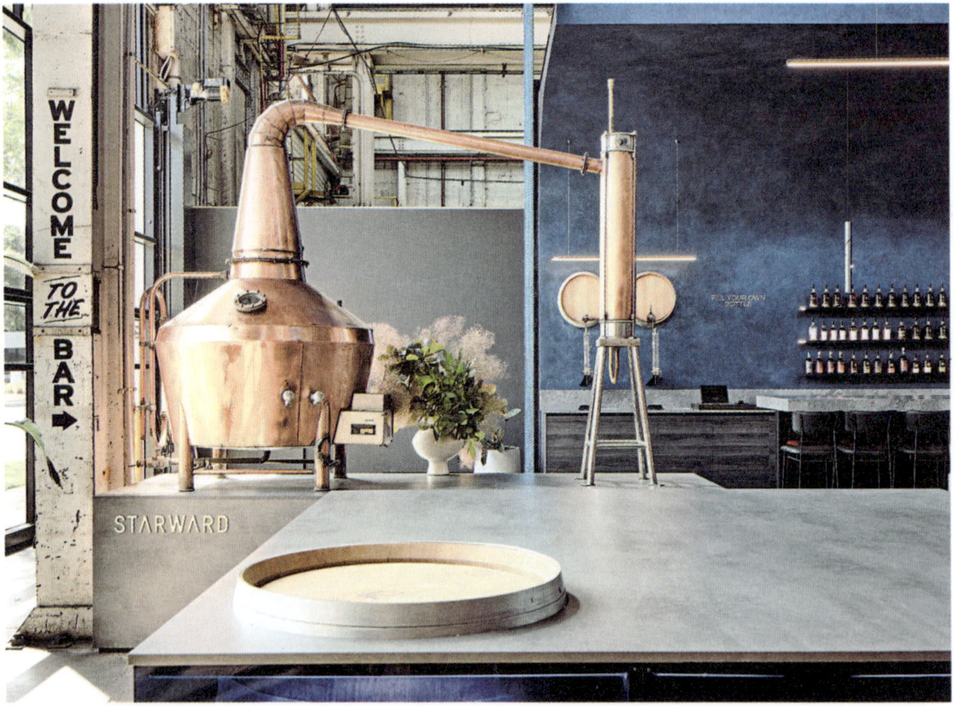
WELCOME
TO THE
BAR
STARWARD

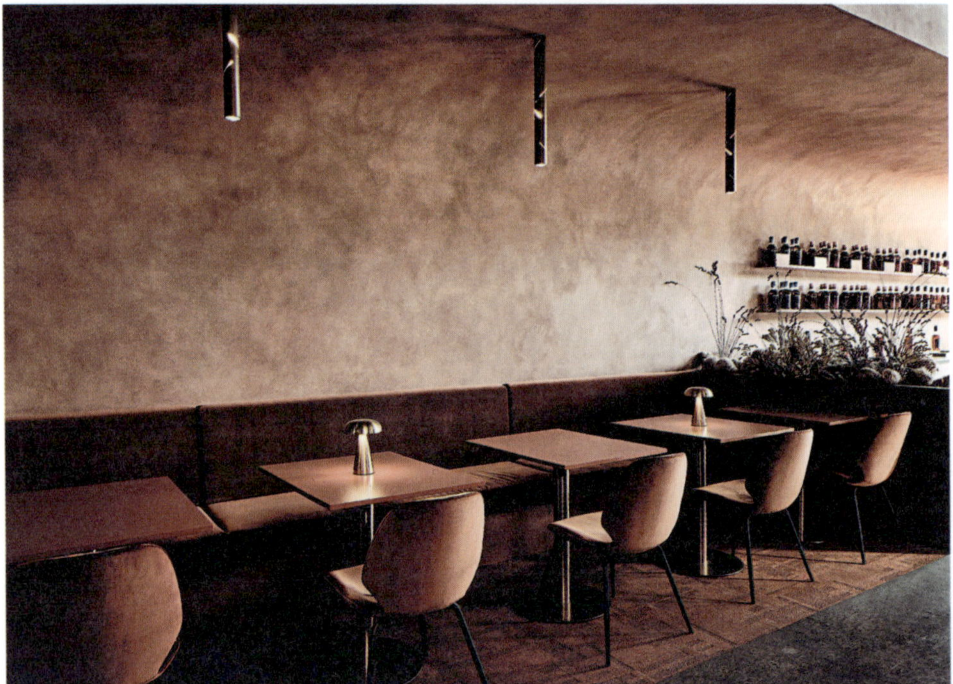

with a unique flavour profile but also formed a direct link between Australia's wine and whisky industries.

The original site of the Starward distillery was in a disused aircraft hangar on the outskirts of Melbourne. With success came a need for a dedicated site, and in 2016 Starward moved to a new facility in Melbourne's Dockland s Precinct, allowing a much more focused visitor experience.

The distillery itself is open Thursday through to Sunday, and offers tours and tastings, as well as a fantastic restaurant, too. There are often events with other producers, such as brewers and wine-makers, and a range of wonderful whisky-based cocktails served at the bar.

What Starward has achieved is remarkable: a whisky not bound by tradition, but liberated by it. It is as if the distillery has captured the restless energy of Australia itself – its innovation, its connection to the land, and its willingness to take risks. In every bottle of Starward, there is the story of a sunburnt country, of vineyards and barley fields, of a distillery that is young yet wise, daring yet rooted in place.

Starward Solera

43% ABV

The nose reveals a gentle honey aroma complemented by notes of cherry drops, cinnamon, nutmeg and candied orange peel. The palate brings a touch more spice, featuring a generous dollop of vanilla and ginger cake. The finish is soft and well-rounded.

Starward Nova

41% ABV

The aroma presents enticing scents of Christmas cake, vanilla and toffee, layered with a hint of bitter dark chocolate. On the palate, a robust foundation of oak spices is enhanced by maple syrup and milk chocolate, while the finish leaves a delightful impression of all these flavours dusted with cinnamon.

46

The Cardrona

2125 CARDRONA VALLEY RD · WĀNAKA 9382 · NEW ZEALAND

In the 21st century, whisky-making has become a global pursuit.
It is made in the far north of Scotland (see Highland Park, page 176), down
to New Zealand. Here, the most southerly distillery around, The
Cardrona distillery welcomes visitors with open arms.

It is not every day that one stumbles upon a distillery nestled high in a remote valley, embraced by the grandeur of mountains and the quiet hum of nature. But then again, The Cardrona distillery is no ordinary place. Set deep in the Southern Alps of New Zealand, in a region famed for its untamed beauty, the distillery is almost a mirage – an unexpected oasis of craftsmanship and devotion in a land better known for sheep farming and adventure sports. Here, the air is brisk, the mountains cast long shadows, and time moves slower, more deliberately, as if nature itself takes pause to appreciate the artistry unfolding in this far-flung corner of the world.

Located near Wanaka, this family-owned distillery has made waves in the world of distilling with its commitment to quality, craftsmanship and the use of locally sourced ingredients. Established in 2015, The Cardrona has quickly gained recognition for producing world-class whisky, gin, vodka and liqueurs that reflect the purity and beauty of their surroundings.

It was Desiree Reid who first dreamed of this place. Her vision was of fine whisky as good as any from Scotland but born of New Zealand's purest ingredients and its storied landscape. Inspired by the craft and dedication found in the great Scotch distilleries, she spent several years studying the art of distilling before embarking on her project. After extensive research, including visiting distilleries around the world, Reid chose the Cardrona Valley as the perfect location to realize her goal. In 2023 the distillery was bought by Inverhouse Distillers. Reid remains on board as the MD.

With snow-capped peaks on the horizon and a sky that seems impossibly vast, the distillery, when first approached, appears more as a farmhouse than a place of industry. The water used in the distillation process flows from the Crown Range, fed by snowmelt, untouched and pure, its journey from mountaintop to valley uninterrupted by human hand.

Once inside, however, there is no mistaking the purpose of this place.

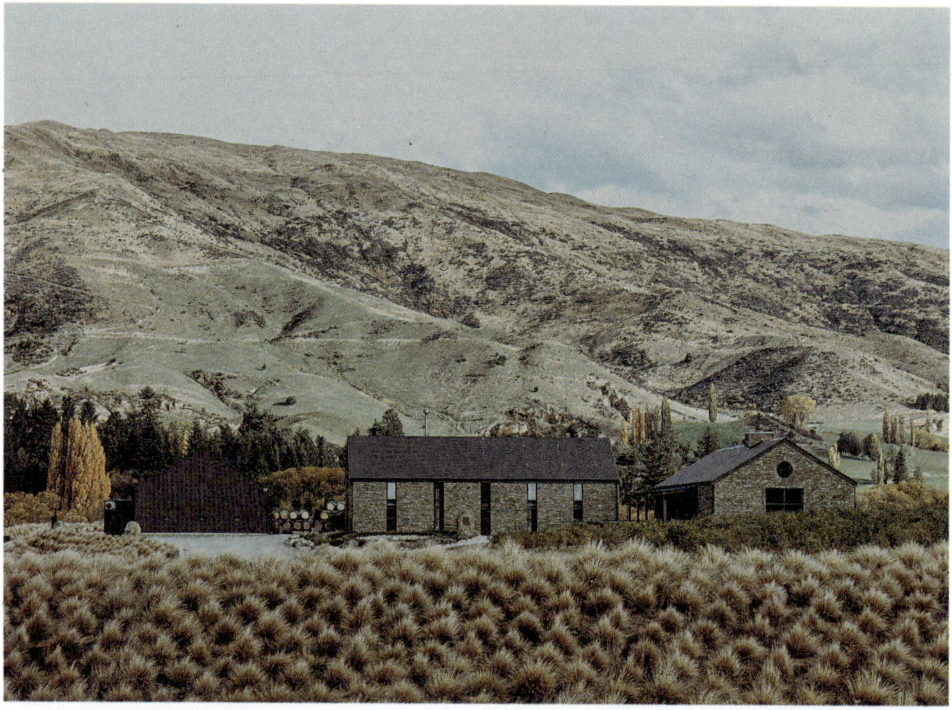

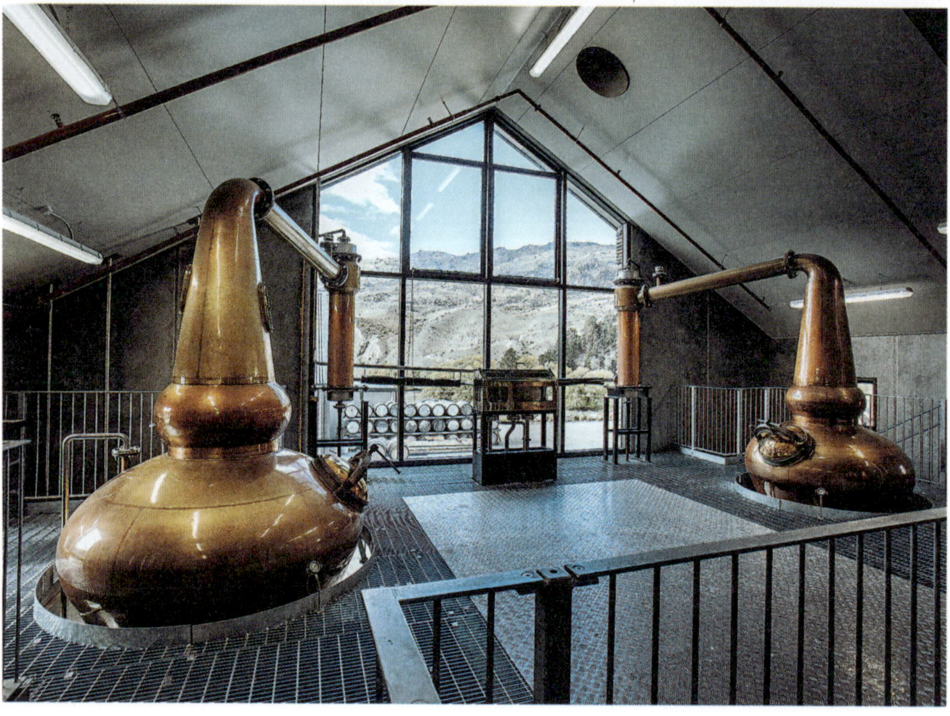

**The Cardrona
The Falcon**

- - - - - - - - - - - - - - - - - - - -

52% ABV

- - - - - - - - - - - - - - - - - - - -

The nose harmoniously blends fruit and spice, dominated by sweet tea, cherry drops and cinnamon. On the palate, the cherry notes are prominent alongside mandarin, complemented by abundant nutmeg and cinnamon that linger well into the finish, where hints of strawberry juice emerge.

Fermentations are long, between three and five days. The two stills (named Roaring Meg and Gentle Annie) were custom-made in Scotland, and stand pointing their lyne arms towards a giant glass wall, and the view of the valley beyond. The distillery also features two other column stills and a small pot still, all used for its gin and vodka production. Maturation is in seasoned oak casks, including Oloroso sherry, bourbon and former pinot noir barriques from Central Otago, New Zealand.

Visiting is encouraged, with The Cardrona's cellar doors open seven days a week, and tours run on the hour from 10am to 3pm. A special 'Cardrona Family Reserve Tour' runs three times a week and lasts for more than three hours, with a deep dive into the distillery and its products.

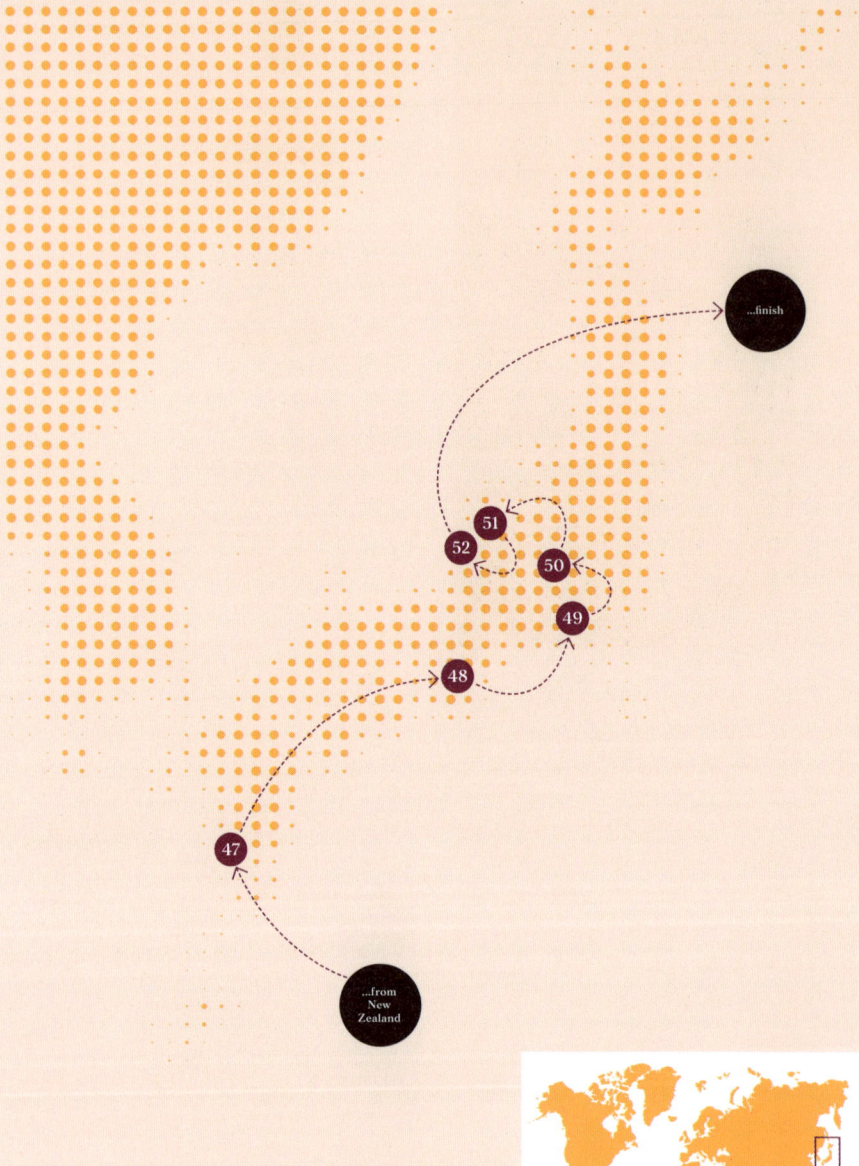

...finish

51
52
50
49
48

47

...from
New
Zealand

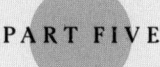

PART FIVE

Japan

A dispatch from Japan

A brief history of Japanese whisky

Fans of Japanese whisky can thank two men for establishing what is today lauded as some of the finest whisky-making in the world. Back in the early 1920s, Taketsuru Masataka and Shinjiro Torii laid the foundations for this globally recognized scene.

The first of these legends, Taketsuru-san, found himself in Scotland studying organic chemistry, and later worked at the Hazelburn distillery in Campbeltown, and the Longmorn distillery in Speyside. His love of Scotch was shared by Torii-san, who owned a drinks company, Suntory, based out of Osaka. Together, they established The Yamazaki distillery (see page 232), high in the Kansai plains, between Kyoto and Osaka, making single malt pot still whisky very much in the Scottish style.

Torii's and Taketsuru's visions for the style of whisky were at odds, with Taketsuru favouring a more smoky single malt, and Torii looking for a more delicate spirit that would mix easily with soda in a Highball. Soon, the pair parted ways with Taketsuru going on to found the Nikka company and the Yoichi distillery in 1934.

Both Suntory and Nikka produce a range of single malts, grain whiskies and blends. Yet, unlike in Scotch where whisky from across the numerous single malt distilleries

is traded freely between the producers and blenders, this is an uncommon practice in Japan. As such, both Suntory and Nikka (and Kirin at the Fuji Gotemba distillery, see page 236) produce a wide range of spirit styles at their distilleries, ensuring they can produce complex blended products.

The Japanese whisky scene is booming.

There are more than 30 distilleries in operation, with more planned. Producers are being encouraged to sign up to a new code of practice with the Japan Spirits & Liqueurs Makers Association (JSLMA). This will ensure that all whisky labelled as Japanese is indeed just that; made and matured in Japan.

This has been put in place to negate the large volumes of whisky imported from Canada, Ireland, America and Scotland, which has in the past been bottled and relabelled as Japanese whisky.

When to visit Japan

Unlike the whisky festivals and trails of Scotland and North America, Japan does not have an organized network of distillery visits or festivities. Therefore, the best time to visit Japan's distilleries is simply whenever you get the chance.

There are advantages to visiting when the weather is fair, and the most beautiful time is undoubtedly during the 'sakura', or cherry blossom season from March to May. However, this is a hugely popular time to visit Japan, and prices can therefore be inflated.

A note on the Highball: where single malt Scotch is often (but not always) consumed neat or on the rocks, and North American whiskey has key serves such as the Old

Fashioned, Whiskey Sour and Manhattan, Japan has made the Highball (whisky, soda and ice) its key serve. Such is the popularity of the Highball that many of the bars will have a whisky Highball on tap, and you can buy cans of it in local supermarkets. The Highball has woven itself into Japanese culture, and you cannot visit the country without trying at least one.

Kanosuke

845-3 HIYOSHICHO KAMINOKAWA · HIOKI · KAGOSHIMA 899-2421 · JAPAN

Kanosuke distillery, located in Kagoshima on Japan's southern island of Kyushu, is one of the country's most exciting new whisky producers. Although the distillery was established in 2017, it is backed by over a century of expertise in spirits production.

In the southern reaches of Japan, where the verdant hills of Kyushu roll toward the sea and the volcanoes brood beneath the clouds, lies a distillery unlike any other. It is not far from the city of Kagoshima, on the edge of a landscape shaped by the whims of nature, that the Kanosuke distillery quietly weaves its story into the annals of Japanese whisky.

The distillery was designed with an ambitious vision: to produce whisky that is uniquely Japanese yet inspired by the craftsmanship of traditional Scottish whisky-making. The distillery prides itself on a highly customized approach to whisky production, paying attention to every stage of the process, from grain selection to fermentation and maturation, even using locally sourced barley.

The distillery uses three pot stills of different shapes and sizes, each designed to create distinct flavour profiles – from traditional double distillation through to triple and part way – a little like Scotland's Springbank distillery (see page 124).

This allows Kanosuke to experiment with a wide range of whisky styles and achieve a complexity that is hard to replicate elsewhere. One of the defining characteristics of Kanosuke whisky is its mellow, rounded flavour, achieved through long fermentation times (nearly a hundred hours) and the use of worm tubs (see page 17).

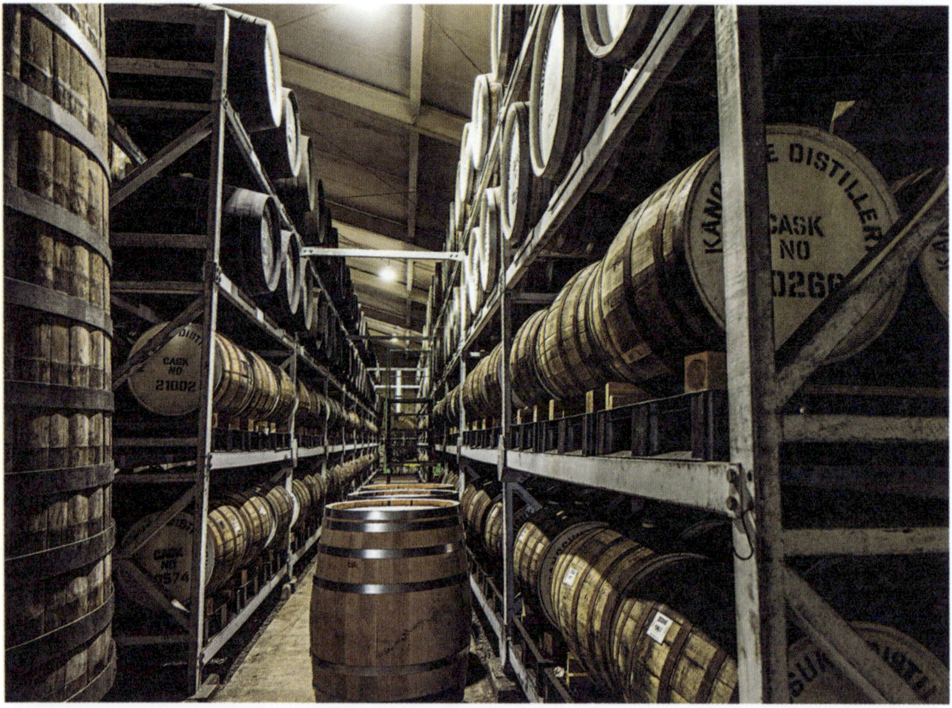
CASK
NO
21002

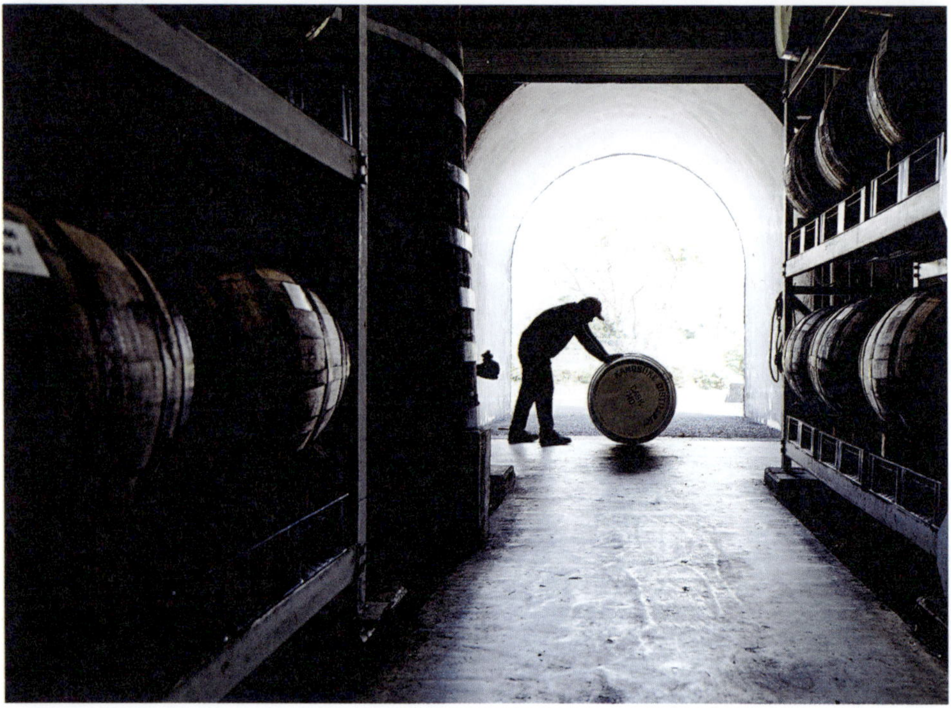

Water quality is crucial in whisky-making, and Kanosuke takes full advantage of its location near Mount Sakurajima, one of Japan's most active volcanoes, with the distillery using fresh groundwater filtered through the volcanic rock. The mineral-rich water is essential for creating the smooth, mellow flavour that Kanosuke whiskies are known for. The proximity to the sea also adds to the distinctive taste, as the maturation process in barrels can be influenced by the coastal air.

Guided tours of the distillery and warehouses are by advance reservation. With expert guides, you will see the whisky-making process up close and enjoy tasting the whisky at the Mellow Bar, overlooking the ocean and a long, white sand beach, on the second floor of the distillery building.

Origins

Komasa Jyozo Co is a company that has been producing traditional Japanese shōchū since 1883 and Kanosuke is a bold venture into whisky-making for a brand steeped in tradition. Komasa Jyozo has always had a long history of fermentation and distillation, and, in 1957, was the first to age shōchū, elevating the drink to a more refined spirit.

For decades, the folk here worked their craft with shōchū, a spirit steeped in the traditions of southern Japan and, in 2017, their craftsmen turned their hands to whisky-making in a dedicated distillery at the site.

Today, Johnnie Walker owner Diageo has invested in the whisky with a view to both plug into the Scotch whisky-maker's expertise, and to expand production, too.

Kanosuke Single Malt

48% ABV

The nose reveals robust malted aromas of pancake batter and an old woodshed, harmoniously balanced by notes of vanilla and subtle rose water. The palate is rich and powerful, featuring flavours of brown bread, malted milk biscuits and dark chocolate, which extend into a long, satisfying finish.

Kanosuke Double Distillery Blended

53% ABV

The nose presents inviting scents of gingerbread, doughnuts and jam, with a hint of smoke. The palate showcases good age, offering a blend of spices and sherry notes, complemented by touches of vanilla. The finish features a gentle smoke at the back, with prominent sherry and spice notes upfront.

48

The Yamazaki

5-2-1 YAMAZAKI · SHIMAMOTO-CHO · MISHIMA-GUN · OSAKA 618-0001 · JAPAN

Nestled in the lush hills between Kyoto and Osaka, The Yamazaki isn't just a distillery; it's the genesis of a new generation of whisky-making, the start of the journey of Japanese single malt and the birthplace of Japanese whisky.

The crisp air in this most verdant part of Japan carries a scent that is part sweet, part smoky, whispering tales of a craft honed over nearly a century. Founded in 1923 by Shinjiro Torii, The Yamazaki was more than just a business idea; it was the manifestation of a vision to create a uniquely Japanese whisky inspired by Scotch. Walking through its gates, you're not just crossing a threshold; you're stepping into history.

The tour begins with an introduction to the man behind the magic. Torii's dream was to create a whisky that would suit the Japanese palate in harmony with Japanese nature. As you meander through the museum-like exhibits, you see his vision unfold. Antique stills, vintage bottles and sepia-toned photographs speak of an era where passion was distilled into every drop.

On the distillery tour itself, the unique process is fully revealed, with the still room the real star. To a backdrop of the slow hiss of distillation, guests are greeted with a collection of different still shapes and sizes. Where most single malt distilleries rely on consistency, which includes the stills, The

Yamazaki is founded on the differences: a gang of stills of varying shapes and sizes, all designed to produce a kaleidoscope of single malt spirit styles.

The sound of fermenting mash, the earthy aroma of malted barley – it's intoxicating even before you've had your first sip. The guide explains the intricacies of the process, from the choice of ingredients to the meticulous ageing in oak barrels. Each step is a testament to the Japanese pursuit of perfection.

Entering the maturation warehouse feels like trespassing into a sacred vault. Rows upon rows of barrels rest in serene silence, each one a promise of liquid gold. The air here is different, saturated with the heady perfume of ageing whisky. It's a cathedral of craftsmanship, where time and patience are the primary artisans.

The distillery itself is a marvel of engineering and tradition. The copper pot stills stand tall like sentinels of tradition, each one playing a crucial role in the whisky-making process. The attention to detail is meticulous. Every inch of the facility

is designed to enhance the quality of the product. The still house, with its gleaming copper and intricate piping, looks like a scene from a Jules Verne fantasy, where old-world charm meets modern precision.

But it's not just the technical aspects that captivate; it's the connection to nature.

The Yamazaki distillery is nestled in a region known for its pure water and ideal climate for whisky production. The surrounding forest and the babbling brooks create a serene backdrop, reminding you that great whisky starts with great natural resources. The distillery's location was chosen with care, ensuring the perfect environment for creating a world-class product.

Throughout the tour, there's a sense of reverence for tradition. The blending room is a sanctum where the blenders work their magic, combining different elements to create a harmonious whole. It's a place of quiet concentration, where years of experience and an innate understanding of flavour come together.

As you leave The Yamazaki, there's a lingering sense of having been a part of something profound. It's more than just whisky; it's a cultural artefact, a testament to Japan's dedication to artistry and excellence. The journey through The Yamazaki is a journey through time and tradition. You carry with you not just a memory of a place, but a deep appreciation for the artistry that turns simple ingredients into something extraordinary.

In the end, visiting The Yamazaki isn't just a tour; it's an exploration of the very heart of Japanese whisky, a journey that lingers long after you've left its tranquil confines.

Origins

The Yamazaki is the OG Japanese whisky distillery, founded in 1923. Combining techniques for traditional Scotch whisky production, including the use of pot stills and sherry cask maturation (the first cask ever filled at The Yamazaki was from Cadiz, in Spain), the whiskies crafted here laid the foundation for the Japanese whisky industry we know today.

The Yamazaki distillery initially struggled to gain recognition as Japanese consumers were unfamiliar with whisky. However, by the mid-20th century, Yamazaki whisky became a symbol of quality and the release of The Yamazaki Single Malt line in the 1980s brought the distillery international acclaim.

It was in the single malt heartlands of Europe and America where the spirit started to win significant awards, and by the early 2000s was lauded as one of the best examples of whisky anywhere in the world. The distillery expanded in 2013, adding four more stills and bringing the total to sixteen, and enabling a capacity increase of over 40 per cent.

It is no understatement to say that The Yamazaki distillery is the keystone of Japanese whisky culture, showcasing the unique artistry of Japanese whisky-making and the flagship ambassador for the category.

The Yamazaki Distiller's Reserve

43% ABV

The Yamazaki Distiller's Reserve is a vibrant and intricate single malt that exemplifies the art of Japanese whisky craftsmanship. Its bright gold hue entices with an aromatic bouquet of red berries, peaches and a hint of coconut. The palate delivers a harmonious fusion of sweet vanilla, honey and citrus zest, beautifully complemented by subtle oak and a whisper of mizunara (Japanese oak) spice. The finish is smooth and refreshing, leaving a lingering impression of fruit and gentle spice.

The Yamazaki 18 Years Old

43% ABV

This whisky presents a deep amber colour, enticing the nose with rich scents of dark chocolate, dried fruits and a touch of smoky oak. The palate unfolds luxuriously, revealing notes of black cherry, sherry-soaked raisins and a hint of espresso, layered with complex spices and a subtle smokiness. The finish is long and elegant, with lasting traces of dark chocolate, dried fruit and a soft whisper of leather. This whisky epitomizes sophistication, providing a deep, balanced and profoundly satisfying experience.

49

Fuji

970 SHIBANTA · GOTEMBA · SHIZUOKA 412-0003 · JAPAN

The Fuji distillery, with a view of Japan's iconic volcano of the same name, was established in 1973. It is part of Japan's burgeoning whisky industry, which has earned global recognition for its craftsmanship and unique approach to production.

There is a place at the foot of Mount Fuji, where the air is crisp and clear, and the great mountain stands watchful, its peak often hidden by clouds, like an ancient god wrapped in mystery. Here, in this serene and almost reverent landscape, lies the Fuji distillery, a monument not only to the art of whisky-making but also to Japan's relationship with its natural surroundings.

The Fuji distillery was founded during a time when Japanese whisky was coming into its own, moving beyond following Scottish whisky-making practice and into its own identity. Kirin, a company known for beer, wanted to expand into the spirits market and chose a site near Mount Fuji for its unique environment. Today, the distillery sits around 620m (2,034ft) above sea level, with a cool climate that closely mirrors the conditions of Scotland. The pure water from Mount Fuji's underground springs is also a crucial factor in the spirit's distinctive character.

The Fuji distillery is unique in its versatility. The distillery produces both malt and grain whiskies, a rare combination that allows it to create a wide variety of styles. In fact, it is one of the few distilleries in the world that can produce both types of whisky onsite. The distillery is equipped with a variety of still types, including pot stills for malt whisky and column stills, kettle stills and doubler stills for grain whisky. This diverse array of equipment allows for exceptional flexibility in crafting a wide range of flavour profiles. Unlike most Japanese distilleries, which follow Scottish whisky-making practices, the Fuji distillery adopts production techniques and methodologies from all over the world. Although the pot stills were modelled on those at the Strathisla distillery in Scotland (see page 144), albeit those at Fuji distillery are bigger in size.

One of the key aspects of the whisky-making process at Fuji is the blending of these different whisky types to create complex, harmonious products. The distillery team is renowned for its ability to balance the characteristics of the malt and

殿場蒸溜所

grain whiskies, resulting in a wide array of styles ranging from delicate and floral to rich and robust, all harmoniously balanced.

The distillery is open every day of the week except for Monday and there is a free shuttle bus from Gotemba station, which leaves roughly every hour for the distillery. The tour kicks off with a presentation on a giant cinema screen. At the end, there is a chance to try the whiskies made onsite, and to take in the view of Mount Fuji and Gotemba city from the rooftop observation deck.

Origins

Established in 1973, the Fuji Gotemba, as it was originally known, was a joint venture between Kirin Brewery Company and North American drinks giant Seagrams. Fuji Gotemba's facilities were designed to integrate diverse whisky production techniques and allow the distillery to create a wide range of whisky styles.

In the 2000s, the distillery gained global recognition as Japanese whisky rose in prominence, bottled under the Kirin name. Today it appears under the Fuji label, and is now fully owned by Kirin.

Fuji Single Blended

46% ABV

The nose is light, opening with grainy notes and a malty core that features olives, vanilla and oak, complemented by a hint of lemon juice. On the palate, vibrant limes and mandarin emerge, creating a delightful sweetness that carries through to the finish, where a touch of liquorice adds intrigue.

Fuji Single Malt

46% ABV

The aroma is rich and buttery, evoking the essence of English cream tea with scones, clotted cream and strawberry jam. The palate reveals notes of pancake batter, rich oak spices and toasted almonds. The finish is marked by rye spices and grain notes, all enveloped in a subtle barbecue smoke.

50

Hakushu

2913-1 TORIHARA · HAKUSHU-CHO · HOKUTO-SHI · YAMANASHI 408-0316 · JAPAN

I've always been a sucker for the kind of place where the soul of a culture reveals itself in every grain and in every bottle and Hakushu distillery, nestled in the Japanese Southern Alps, is exactly that kind of place.

Visitors to Hakushu distillery are in for something very special indeed. Something extraordinary, in fact. For Hakushu is no ordinary distillery; it is a pilgrimage for whisky lovers, a testament to the meticulous craftsmanship of Japanese whisky-making, and mountain dew in a bottle. Hakushu isn't just about whisky; it's about a symphony of elements.

Surrounded by the untouched beauty of Japan's lush, mountainous terrain, the landscape is an expanse of cedar and pine. From afar, it is all deep greens that feel almost otherworldly: part Tolkein's Middle-earth, part Game of Thrones' Eyrie. Here, mist hangs from the hills like cotton wool.

Hakushu, unlike any other distillery, produces a single malt that reflects the land it calls home. A mountain forest distillery in the Japanese Southern Alps, it is a seamless blend of natural beauty and masterful artistry; Shinrin-yoku, 'forest bathing', in a glass. Key to this is the water source, which is famed in Japan and sold as bottled drinking water. It comes from snowmelt that trickles through granite on its way to the distillery.

The distillery is located in the Yamanashi Prefecture at the foot of Mount Kaikoma. On arrival (regular free buses are on offer from the local railway station, two hours away from the madness of Tokyo), visitors are led up a forest path that weaves through a bird sanctuary, where various species of flora and fauna are picked out by information signs before a welcome centre and shop.

Once at the distillery, there is a welcoming restaurant, Hakushu Terrace, which opened in 2024 and serves fantastic pizza and delicious Japanese fried chicken. And Hakushu Highballs, of course!

The distillery is split into two parts: one ghosted and silent, the other quietly getting on with life. In the former (viewable on the Monozukuri Prestige tour), huge black copper stills – decommissioned in 1995 – sit as statues to the development of Japanese whisky over the last two decades. The new still house, much like The Yamazaki (see page 232) is an eclectic selection of shapes and sizes: small stills producing heavy spirit and taller, elegant varieties making a lighter style of single malt.

The tours will take you around the production process (save for the old still house) and start with a simple, multimedia overview of whisky-making. The conclusion of the tour allows a second distillery visitor's centre shop to be raided, and its miniature distillery edition offering is worth the visit alone. The tasting lounge offers a range of drams from across the Hakushu range, as well as blends from owner Suntory's portfolio. Food and drink pairings are also available.

The signature Hakushu Single Malt is crisp and refreshing with a smoky complexity that lingers; balanced with a subtle smokiness that's neither overpowering nor intrusive. It's a whisky that embodies its environment, a liquid representation of the alpine freshness that surrounds the distillery.

Origins

Hakushu was built by by Keizo Saji, the second president and second master blender of Suntory, in 1973 to complement the style of whisky made at its other single malt plant, The Yamazaki (see page 232). Constructed 50 years after work started on The Yamazaki, it marked an important milestone in Japan's rise as a world-class whisky producer.

The old still house – known today as Monozukuri Building – was decommissioned in 1995. It started life, however, with six pairs of stills and, by the early 1980s, it was the biggest single malt distillery in the world. In 1981, the distillery expanded once more with the construction of the current distillation area, slowly running down the operation in the older development, which is now home to a variety of different size and type of pot stills that aim to create diverse whiskies. In late 2010 Suntory opened a small grain distillery on the site. Floor maltings (see page 17) are also in operation now, having been revived in 2024.

The Hakushu Distiller's Reserve

43% ABV

The nose opens with delicate notes of cigarillo smoke. On the palate, you'll find savoury bacon bits intertwined with lovely floral peat smoke, complemented by oak spices, a hint of leather polish and chamois leather. The finish is brief yet carries a spicy tone.

The Hakushu 12 Years Old

43% ABV

The aroma is malt-forward, showcasing abundant oak and floral smoke, along with hints of coconut and dry spice. The palate is beautifully balanced, featuring notes of cereal, dark chocolate and hazelnuts. The finish reveals leather and the scent of old books, reflecting the whisky's age.

51

Miyagikyo

1 NIKKA · AOBA WARD · SENDAI · MIYAGI 989-3433 · JAPAN

The Miyagikyo distillery, located in the picturesque mountains of Sendai in Japan's Miyagi Prefecture, is one of the most renowned whisky distilleries in the world. Established in 1967 by Masataka Taketsuru, the founder of Nikka Whisky, Miyagikyo is the second distillery of the Nikka company, complementing the Yoichi distillery in Hokkaido.

Miyagikyo is set in a lush, green valley between the Nikkawa and Hirose rivers. The site was carefully chosen by Taketsuru due to its clean, soft water and ideal climate with the surrounding forests and mountains, which offer a temperate climate with high humidity, providing ideal conditions for maturing whisky.

One of the most important elements of Miyagikyo's whisky is the water sourced from the rivers flowing through the area. This water is soft, in contrast to the harder, mineral-rich water found at Yoichi. The softness of the water plays a crucial role in the lighter, more elegant style of whisky produced at Miyagikyo, contributing to its delicate and floral characteristics.

While the Yoichi distillery is known for its robust, peaty and smoky whiskies, Miyagikyo is famous for producing lighter, fruitier and more refined spirits. Larger pot stills are employed, with indirect steam heating, which helps create a lighter and more delicate spirit and is designed to

preserve the fruity and floral notes in the whisky, and the slow distillation process ensures that these qualities are fully developed.

In addition to producing single malt whiskies, Miyagikyo distils grain whisky, which is used in Nikka's blended whiskies. The distillery operates Coffey stills, which

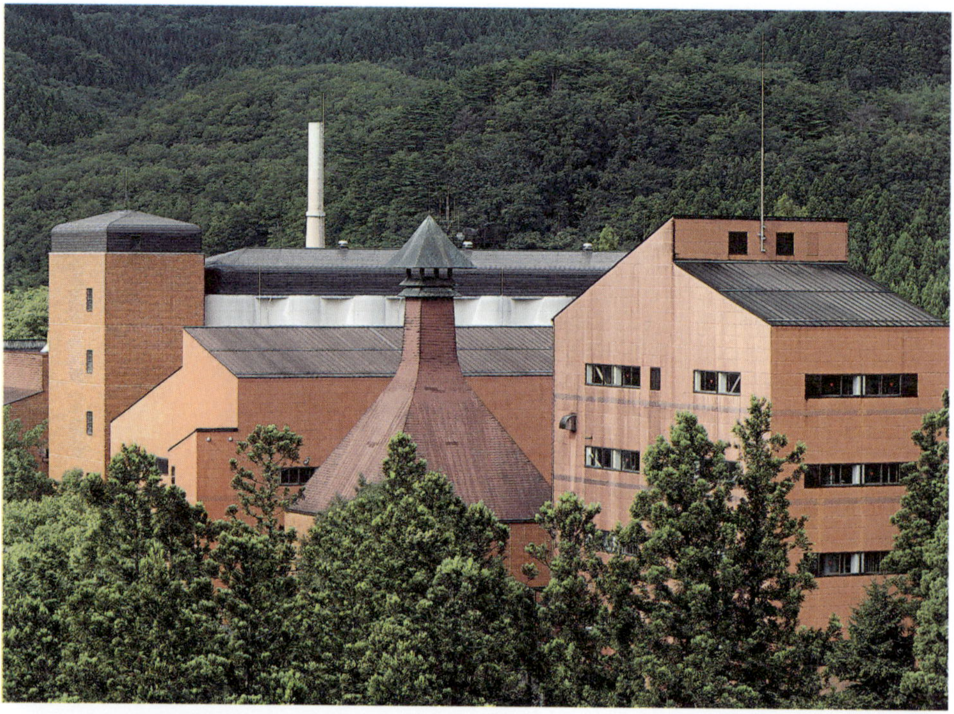

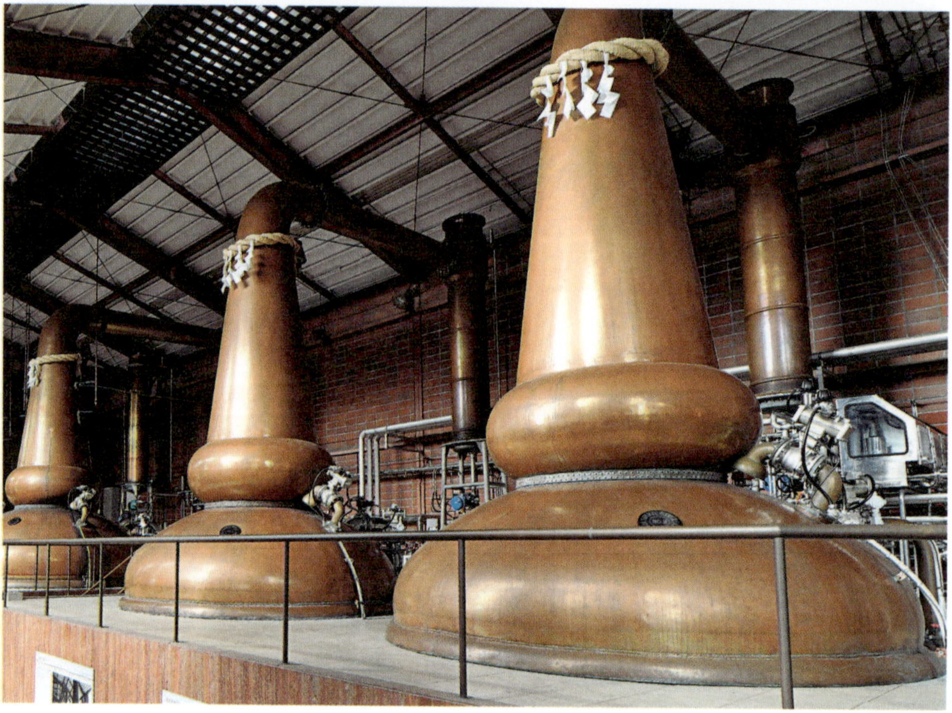

were imported from Scotland in the 1960s, and are an integral part of the production process at Miyagikyo, allowing the distillery to create high-quality grain whisky. The combination of single malt and grain whisky gives parent company Nikka the ability to create complex and well-balanced blends.

Tours are by reservation only, and take in the whole whisky-making process, concluding with a tasting. They are free and last just over an hour. It takes just under two hours on the bullet train from Tokyo to Sendai station, before an hour in a free shuttle bus, or another 40 minutes aboard a local train to Sakunami station and a 25 minute walk from there. There is another free shuttle bus from this closer railway station but only on Fridays, Saturdays and Sundays.

Origins

Miyagikyo was founded in 1967 by Masataka Taketsuru (see page 226), who played an instrumental role in establishing Japan's whisky industry. As his whisky-making journey continued, Taketsuru envisioned creating another distillery that could produce a different style of whisky to his first, Yoichi (see page 248) and commissioned family member Takeshi Taketsuru to find a site for a second facility.

It is believed to have taken Taketsuru three years to find the site for this distillery in the scenic valley near Sendai but, once the site was identified, the distillery was built and operational within two years.

Today, it appears as a single malt, but the product is also a key component in the blends within the Nikka whisky portfolio.

Miyagikyo
Single Malt

45% ABV

There are sweet notes of Battenberg cake and green tea, with a hint of vanilla on the nose. The palate is malty and oaky with a blast of roasted chestnuts and some vanilla, too. These are all in the finish, with a hint of blackcurrant leaf.

52

Yoichi

7 CHOME-6 · KUROKAWACHO · YOICHI · YOICHI DISTRICT · 046-0003 HOKKAIDO · JAPAN

The Yoichi distillery, on the northern island of Hokkaido, is a place where tradition, craft and nature come together to create one of Japan's most revered whiskies. Yoichi has earned a reputation for producing robust, peaty and full-bodied whiskies that capture the wild spirit of the northern Japanese coast.

Situated near the town of Yoichi, the distillery is surrounded by mountains to the east and the Sea of Japan to the west. This rugged, coastal environment plays a crucial role in the whisky-making process, with the cool, humid climate and salty sea air imparting distinctive flavours to the spirit.

One of the most distinctive features of Yoichi's whisky-making process is its use of coal-fired pot stills, a method that has all but disappeared from modern distilleries. In most, pot stills are heated using steam, which provides a more controlled and even heat. With direct coal flames, a technique largely abandoned, the coal fire produces a hotter, more intense heat, which gives the whisky a distinctive, rich character. This method, while labour-intensive and challenging to manage, is one of the reasons Yoichi whiskies are known for bold, full-bodied flavours.

Visitors are welcome with a prior booking, but Yoichi is not a place you happen upon. You must go looking for it, as Taketsuru did. It is just over an hour from Sapporo

station by local train, and the distillery also features the Nikka Museum, which opened in October 2021. The museum is a tour facility where you can experience Nikka's whisky through exhibits with a

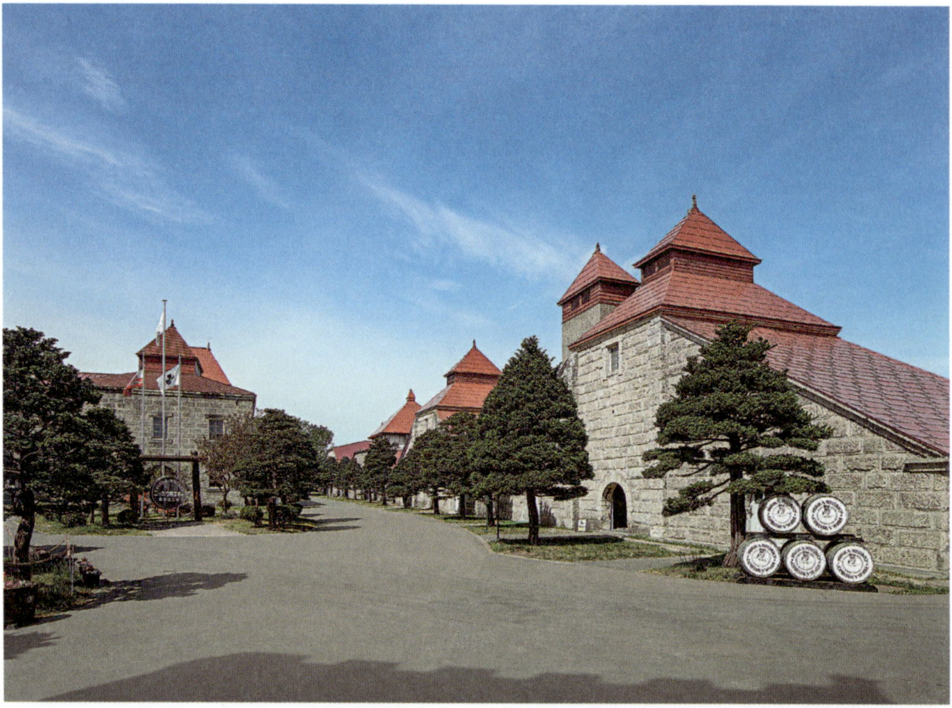

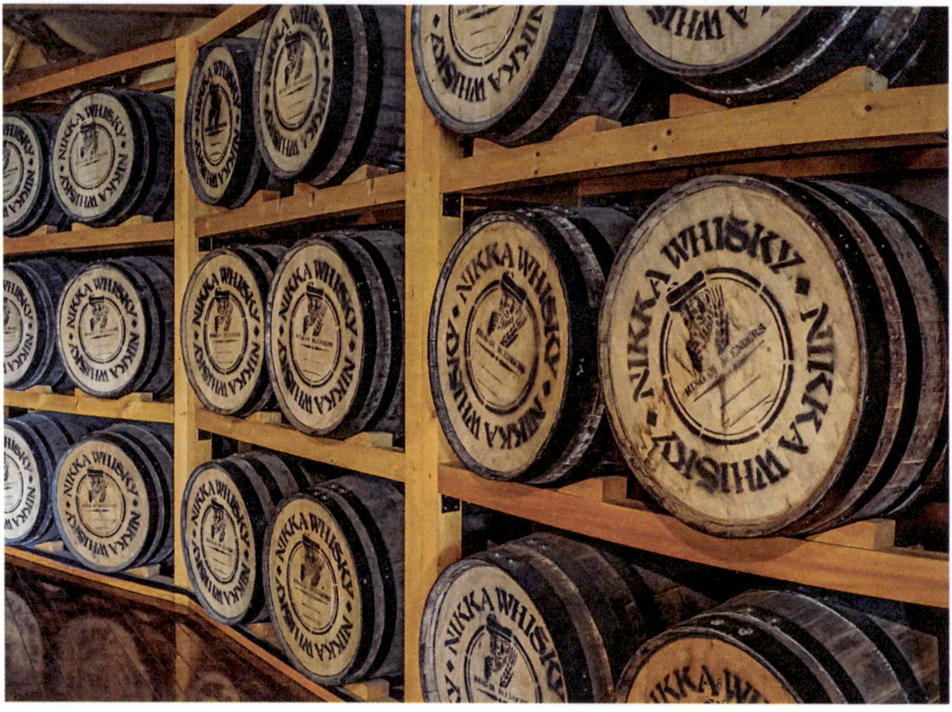
NIKKA WHISKY

special focus on blending. There is also a wonderful restaurant, Rita's Kitchen (named after Taketsuru's Scottish wife), which serves British and Scottish cuisine, as well as dishes and drinks that feature ingredients from Hokkaido.

Origins

It could be the rugged, maritime location and commitment to traditional whisky-making techniques that gives Yoichi's whisky such an elemental flavour. But, more likely, it is the vision of founder Masataka Taketsuru.

Taketsuru journeyed to Scotland in the early 20th century to learn the secrets of whisky-making, and found himself working in Campbeltown (see page 111) which at the time was famed for its bold, oily, smoky and robust single malts.

After returning to Japan, Taketsuru-san was determined to bring this style of authentic Scotch-style whisky to his homeland. He first worked for Suntory, helping to establish Japan's first whisky distillery at The Yamazaki, near Kyoto. But his style of whisky was too smoky for his then business partner, Shinjiro Torii.

Taketsuru's vision was more specific. He wanted to build a distillery that would produce the bold, smoky whiskies he had come to love. In 1934, he left Suntory and set out on his own, eventually founding the Nikka Whisky company and establishing the Yoichi distillery on Hokkaido, and latterly the Miyagikyo distillery (see page 244).

Yoichi Single Malt

45% ABV

A rich and robust nose features summer fruits and jams, complemented by subtle hints of oud and cinnamon. The palate is equally smooth and decadent, showcasing toasted sourdough bread, dark chocolate, a dash of sea salt and a drizzle of mānuka honey. The finish is long and spiced, with a gentle touch of vanilla sweetness.

Index

Picture credits

We would like to thank all the distilleries and their agents who have so kindly sent us images for use in this book.

Amrut Distilleries Ltd 205, all 206, 207; **Ardbeg Distillery** 114b, 115r, photo Ben Shakespeare 114a, photo Sim Canetty-Clarke 115l; **Auchentoshan,** Suntory Global Spirits 133, 134a & b, all 135; **Balcones Distilling** 30, 31, all 32, 33; **Bowmore,** Edrington 121, 122a & b, 123; **Buffalo Trace Distillery** all 40, all 41; **Bushmills Irish Whiskey** 105, photo Bradley Quinn 103, 104b; **Cardrona Distillery** 221, 222a & b, 223; **Cotswolds Distillery** 185, all 186, 187l & r; **Diageo** 117, 118a & b, 119, 130a, 131r, 137, 139r, photo Graeme Mac-Donald 139l, photo Simon Hird 138b; **Domaine des Hautes Glaces** 191, photos Céline Clanet 189, 190a & b; **Forty Creek,** Campari Group 75, 76a & bl, 77; **Fuji Gotemba,** Kirin Brewery Company 237, all 238, 239; **Glenmorangie** 175l & r, photo Carol Sachs 174a, photo Paul Wilkinson 173, photo Sim Canetty-Clarke 174b; **Hakushu,** Suntory Global Spirits 241, 242a & b, 243r; **Highland Park** 177, all 178, 179; **Irish Distillers,** Pernod Ricard 85, 97; **Jack Daniels,** Brown-Forman 67, 68a & b, 69; **James Sedgwick Distillery,** Heineken 200, 201, all 202, 203; **Jim Beam,** Suntory Global Spirits 53l & r; **Kanosuke** 228, 229, 230a, 231, photo Kato Shu 230b; **Kavalan Distillery,** King Car Group 212, 213, 214a & b, 215; **Maker's Mark Distillery,** Suntory Global 35, 37; **Nearest Green Distillery** 71, 73, photo Amy Haring 72a, photo Stacy Preston 72b; **Nikka Whisky** 244, 246a, 247, 248, 250a, 251; **Old Forester,** Brown-Forman 58, 59, all 60, all 61; **Pernod Ricard** 211r; **Rabbit Hole,** Pernod Ricard 47, all 48, 49; **Roe & Co** 93, photo Christopher Heaney 91, 92a & b; **Slyrs Distillery,** all 193, 194, 195; **Springbank Distillers Ltd** 13, 127r, photo From Barrel to Bottle 125, Erik Ritchie/From Barrel to Bottle 126a & b; **Starward** 216, 217, 218a & b, all 219; **Stauning Whisky** 196, 197, all 198, 199; **Stranahan's** 28a & b, 29; **Strathisla,**

Pernod Ricard 147; **Teeling Whiskey** 87, 89r, photo Zima Photos 88bl; **The Balvenie** 153, all 154, 155r, photo John Paul 155l; **The Bardstown Bourbon Company** 5, 56a & b, 57; **The Dalmore** 171, photo Andy Taylor 170bl; **The Glen Grant** 161, 162a & b, 163; **The Glenfiddich** 151r; **The Glenlivet,** Pernod Ricard 167r, photo John Paul 166a & b, 167l; **The Glenturret** 142a & b, 143r, photo Marc Millar 141, 143l; **The Macallan** 159, photo Ian Gavan 158b; **Tullamore D.E.W.** 101, photo Jeff Harvey 100b, photo Tristan Hutchinson 99a; **Wild Turkey,** Campari Group 19, 63, all 64, 65; **Woodford Reserve,** 43, 44a & b, 45; **Yamazaki,** Suntory Global Spirits 226, 227, 233, 234a, 235.

Additional photography:

Alamy Stock Photo Ketaro Aoyama/Associated Press 245, Caroline Chen/Associated Press 210bl, CNMages 52b, Daniel Dempster Photography 15, 39, Horst Friedrichs 18, 127l, 145br, 146 a & bl, Hugh Mitton 130b, 131l, Imago Images/Xinhua 210a, Jasper Image 150a, John Bracegirdle 149, 157, 158a, 165, Jon Arnold 94, Littleny 52a, Lori Barbely 96, Malcolm Walker 83, Masamine Kawaguchi/Associated Press 249, Media World Images 170a, Serge Connu 138a, Vitalli 95, wanderluster 36b, Will Dale 129, Woodsnorth Photography 51, Yoshikazu Okunishi/Associated Press 246b; **Andrew Montgomery** for Octopus Publishing 6; **Cathal Noonan** 84a & b; **John Fink**/Flickr (CC by 2.0) 76br; **Getty Images** Akio Kon/Bloomberg via Getty Images 234b, John Sommers II/Bloomberg via Getty Images 36a, Martin Fraser 110, Qilai Shen/Bloomberg via Getty Images 17, 183, 209, 210br, 211l, SSPL 80, Stefano Guidi 89l; **iStock** lucentius 145, 169, Lukassek 113, Wirestock 88a; **Joel Harrison** 2, 8, 9 23, 24, 81, 109, 111; **Shutterstock** Andy Sutherland 88 br, Geoff Moore 44br, Infinite_Eye 27, 291, Travelling Tourist 150b, 151l.

Acknowledgements

Dedicated to my late uncle, Tor Visnes. Sorry we didn't get to visit some of these places together.

I would like to thank each and every person who has helped bring this book to life. A legion of distillers, blenders, marketeers, brand ambassadors and PR folk from around the world, all who love this industry as much as I do. This book would have been impossible without you all.

A special thank you to Charlie MacLean for his wonderful foreword, and ongoing wisdom and advice.

To the team at Octopus: Alison Starling, Jeannie Stanley, Pauline Bache, Jonathan Christie, Matt Grindon and Megan Brown. You are all consistently excellent. And to my agent, Martine Carter at Sauce Management.

Other thanks to Nick Dudley-Williams, Nick Gatfield and Neil Ridley. To Hamish and Pip Denny at the Shamble Bar, Windsor for the constant flow of cocktails. To Chris Matthews and James Windle for the football chat, as well as Ken Grier, Timmy Mallett and Arthur Motley, Richard Norridge and Andy Silvester, too.

To my parents, Stuart and Sissel Harrison. Thank you.

The biggest thanks of all goes to my wife, Victoria Grier, for her constant support.

First published in Great Britain in 2025
by Mitchell Beazley, an imprint of
Octopus Publishing Group Ltd, Carmelite House, 50
Victoria Embankment, London EC4Y 0DZ
www.octopusbooks.co.uk

An Hachette UK Company
www.hachette.co.uk

The authorized representative in the EEA is Hachette Ireland, 8 Castlecourt Centre, Dublin 15, D15 XTP3, Ireland (email: info@hbgi.ie)

Text copyright © Joel Harrison 2025
Design and layout copyright
© Octopus Publishing Group 2025

Endpapers photograph courtesy of Highland Park

Distributed in the US by Hachette Book Group, 1290 Avenue of the Americas, 4th and 5th Floors, New York, NY 10104

Distributed in Canada by Canadian Manda Group, 664 Annette St., Toronto, Ontario, Canada M6S 2C8

ISBN 978-1-78472-965-3

A CIP catalogue record for this book is available from the British Library.

Printed and bound in Dubai

10 9 8 7 6 5 4 3 2 1

Commissioning editor: Jeannie Stanley
Creative director: Jonathan Christie
Senior developmental editor: Pauline Bache
Copyeditor: Molly Price
Picture research managers: Giulia Hetherington and Jennifer Veal
Assistant production manager: Lisa Pinnell